MW01595867

Learn God's Word

Receive His Rewards

by

Dr. Jerry Kirchner

The McDougal Publishing Company

PUBLISHED BY:

The McDougal Publishing Company
P.O. Box 3595
Hagerstown, MD 21742-3595

ISBN 1-884369-14-6

Printed in the United States of America
For Worldwide Distribution

DEDICATION

We would like to dedicate this book to all who are seekers after truth. Those who are willing to search the Word of God for the treasures that are found within its pages so that they might be more effective witnesses of His truths.

And I will give them the treasures of darkness and hidden riches of secret places that thou mayest know that I the Lord which call thee by thy name am the God of Israel. Isaiah 45:3

Seek the Lord while He may be found, call upon Him while He is near. Let the wicked forsake His way and the unrighteous man His thoughts.
Isaiah 55:6-11

ACKNOWLEDGMENTS

Many thanks to those who helped me to organize this material. To Jael Tung Boh Lai, who typed my manuscript into the computer, a special thanks for the hours of labor she willingly offered to help us. To my wife Ginny, who read and reread through the material to offer invaluable contributions and corrections. To Harold McDougal, who has been our editor for all of our books. Without his able assistance we could not have efficiently produced any of our writing. To each of you, thanks, and God bless you!

CONTENTS

Introduction

1. Learn That God's Ways Are Always Best 1
2. Learn To Hear the Voice of God 9
3. Learn To Fight Fear With Faith 17
4. Learn To Be Stubborn In Your Resolve 33
5. Learn To Practice What You Preach 45
6. Learn To Put the Natural Man In His Place . 49
7. Learn To Stay Humble 55
8. Learn What Pleases God 65
9. Learn To Appreciate the Love of God 81
10. Learn the Power of Words 89
11. Learn the Importance of Work 103
12. Learn To Avoid Spiritual Blindness 119
13. Learn The Source of All Knowledge and
    Power 135
14. Learn To Be Faithful 149
15. Ever Learning 155

INTRODUCTION

We are living in such exciting and challenging times. Before our very eyes, the world is changing, and those changes present to us, as ministers of the Gospel and people of God in general, opportunities that we have never known before, opportunities that are unique in world history.

Suddenly, the greatest mission field in the world is not Africa or China or even India, but the former Soviet block nations, and desperate calls are going out from there for anyone who will come and help the people to reestablish the moral base destroyed by seventy years of Communism.

But these are not the only open doors. Suddenly, doors of opportunity have flung open in every corner of the globe, and there is no lack of prospects for ministry. In fact, there is a desperate cry in many areas for *qualified* people to heed the call for help.

This call may seem to be coming from people, but just as the Macedonian was used of God to speak to the Apostle Paul in his dream, God is using the desperation of the nations to call forth His people to reach out to men and women in need of the Good News of the Gospel and to reap a harvest of souls while there is yet time.

When we talk about those whom the Lord can use, the key word is *"qualified."* Many people love our Lord Jesus and want to serve Him, but they are not *qualified* to do so because they have missed opportunities to prepare themselves adequately, to sit at the Master's feet and receive from Him so that they could go forth and give out to others. We cannot bless others if we have not first been blessed ourselves. We cannot teach others if we have not first learned what we are attempting to teach. We cannot lead others into experiences that we have not had ourselves.

Jesus spent many hours teaching His disciples. He taught them through parables, through exhortation of the Scriptures, and also through practical experience. Just being with Him was an education.

The need to learn the ways of God did not begin with the disciples. Abraham, Isaac and Jacob had important lessons to learn that made them so qualified that we remember them as "the patriarchs." Moses and Joshua had much to learn to lead such a great people out of Egypt, across the desert and into the promised land.

Elijah and Elisha, Isaiah, Jeremiah, Ezekiel, Daniel and all the other prophets of Israel, both known and unknown, were prophets because of what they had learned about God and were able to share with others.

Even the kings, beginning with Saul and David, had much to learn to enable them to govern effectively and with God's favor upon them and the people they led.

Personally, the more I learn about God, the more I realize that I need to learn. And, as the challenges of ministry increase, I realize the need to reach out to God for new lessons of faith and trust, new lessons of relationship, so that I can continue to be effective for Him.

Recently, God has been showing me some of the basic lessons He taught His servants, beginning with the Patriarchs and continuing with the kings, the prophets, and the disciples of the New Testament. These are lessons that will bless all of us and bring us into a deeper place with God so that we might serve Him better. Let us learn them so that we can accept the challenges of our present day and so that we will be prepared for the greater things God has for us in the future. *"It is time to seek the Lord,"* (Hosea 10:12).

Dr. Jerry Kirchner
Route 1, Box 365
Ashland, VA 23005

- 1 -

LEARN THAT GOD'S WAYS ARE ALWAYS BEST

Now Sarai Abram's wife bare him no children: and she had an handmaid, an Egyptian, whose name was Hagar. And Sarai said unto Abram, Behold now, the Lord hath restrained me from bearing: I pray thee, go in unto my maid; it may be that I may obtain children by her. And Abram hearkened to the voice of Sarai.

Genesis 16:1-2

By not waiting on God, and by taking things into their own hands, Abraham and Sarah brought heartache upon their own marriage and adversely affected the future course of history for their descendants.

God had promised them that they would have descendants *"as the dust of the earth," "as the stars of the heaven,"* and *"as the sand which is upon the sea shore."*

> *I will make thy seed as the dust of the earth: so that if a man can number the dust of the earth, then shall thy seed also be numbered.*
>
> Genesis 13:16

> *In blessing I will bless thee, and in multiplying I will multiply thy seed as the stars of the heaven, and as the sand which is upon the sea shore; and thy seed shall possess the gate of his enemies;*
>
> Genesis 22:17

When years passed and Abraham and Sarah could not see any evidence that God was working to perform His promise, they decided to take things into their own hands. There would be a child, an heir, — by *their* method. Sarah would give her maid, Hagar, to Abraham, and he would have a child by her — as was the custom of the day.

What a sad chapter in the life of these two great people of faith! When God says He will do something, we can bank on it. He never fails; His promises are sure; and He doesn't need our help to accomplish His work.

Abraham was a man of faith, the very father of faith, and if a story of his failure in this regard is included in the Bible, it must have an important purpose. This story should be a warning to each of us not to fall into the kind of thinking that caused Abraham and Sarah to move outside the will of God for their lives.

For most of his life, Abraham served as a model of great faith and trust in God. Nowhere is this more dramatically revealed than when God called upon him to sacrifice his own son, Isaac.

> *And he said, Take now thy son, thine only son Isaac, whom thou lovest, and get thee into the land of Moriah; and offer him there for a burnt offering upon one of the mountains which I will tell thee of.*   Genesis 22:2

What a test of faith! This was the most serious test of faith that any of us could have devised for the old patriarch, for he had waited almost a hundred years for his "child of promise." Was it too much for God to ask that he now give back the one thing in the world that was most precious to him?

The amazing thing about this story is that, in reading the scriptural account, we cannot notice even a hint of rebelliousness on the part of Abraham. He did not question God on the matter, and he did not hesitate, as most of us would have done, looking for a way to avoid obeying.

We can only imagine what a struggle Abraham must have gone through in his own soul as he carried out God's instructions. We can only imagine the thoughts that must have run through his mind as he took his journey and got ever closer to Moriah, the place of execution. Such a battle of soul and mind would have torn many of us apart.

Do we imagine that the devil, out of respect for Abraham, would have left him alone? Not for a moment! There can be no doubt that Satan badgered Abraham every step of the way.

> *What kind of God would do such a despicable thing?*
> *What kind of God would take back the very thing He promised so long ago?*
> *What kind of God would take the thing you love most and leave you with no heir and no future?*
> *If God is going to turn His back on you, you should turn your back on Him.*

How do we know the devil said such things? Because he never misses an opportunity to try God's children and to accuse God before them and them before God. He is *"the accuser of the brethren."*

> *And I heard a loud voice saying in heaven, Now is come salvation, and strength, and the kingdom of our God, and the power of his Christ: for THE ACCUSER OF OUR BRETHREN is cast down, which accused them before our God day and night.*   Revelation 12:10

Lucifer had shown from the beginning his quickness to criticize God:

Now the serpent was more subtil than any beast of the field which the Lord God had made. And he said unto the woman, Yea, hath God said, Ye shall not eat of every tree of the garden? And the woman said unto the serpent, We may eat of the fruit of the trees of the garden: But of the fruit of the tree which is in the midst of the garden, God hath said, Ye shall not eat of it, neither shall ye touch it, lest ye die. And the serpent said unto the woman, Ye shall not surely die: For God doth know that in the day ye eat thereof, then your eyes shall be opened, and ye shall be as gods, knowing good and evil.   Genesis 3:1-5

And Satan has never changed. This is still his tactic today.

But Abraham was not fooled. He pressed on toward obedience on Mt. Moriah and, thus, earned forever the title *"Father of Faith."*

And he received the sign of circumcision, a seal of the righteousness of the faith which he had yet being uncircumcised: that he might be the father of all them that believe, though they be not circumcised; that righteousness might be imputed unto them also: And the father of circumcision to them who are not of the circumcision only,

but who also walk in the steps of that faith of our
father Abraham, which he had being yet uncir-
cumcised.   Romans 4:11-12

In the case of the sacrifice of Isaac, Abraham's faith
was proven when he declared to those who accompanied him that he and the child would go to the
mountain to worship and would return.

And Abraham said unto his young men, Abide
ye here with the ass; and I and the lad will go
yonder and worship, and come again to you.
                                        Genesis 22:5

Abraham knew that he was about to sacrifice His
son (at God's command). Yet he knew that God is
good and that everything God declares is for a purpose and for our ultimate benefit, never for our
detriment. His faith, thus, led him to believe that, in
the end, Isaac would live. *If God takes Isaac's life,* he
reasoned in his heart, *He can easily restore it.* No human in the Bible faced a greater trial, and no human
in the Bible showed more faith and courage.

It was only at the final moment, when Abraham
had his hand raised, ready to plunge the dagger into
his son, that God showed forth His great love and
compassion, and in doing so revealed His plan of
salvation for men of all ages.

And Abraham stretched forth his hand, and took
the knife to slay his son. And the angel of the

*Lord called unto him out of heaven, and said,
Abraham, Abraham: and he said, Here am I.
And he said, Lay not thine hand upon the lad,
neither do thou any thing unto him: for now I
know that thou fearest God, seeing thou hast not
withheld thy son, thine only son from me. And
Abraham lifted up his eyes, and looked, and behold behind him a ram caught in a thicket by his
horns: and Abraham went and took the ram, and
offered him up for a burnt offering in the stead of
his son.*   Genesis 22:10-13

God spared Isaac when He saw that Abraham was
willing to give back even his most precious possession, that Abraham's love for God and his obedience
to God were the motivating factors in his life, nothing else.

Abraham's submission to the will of God in this
regard foreshadowed the time when the Father
would offer up His only Son on Mt. Calvary. In this
case, He did not stay the hand of the executioner, but
gave all because He loved all.

*For God so loved the world, that he gave his only
begotten Son, that whosoever believeth in him
should not perish, but have everlasting life.*
     John 3:16

When we consider the sacrifice of Jesus for our
sins, our own problems in life, whatever they might
be, fade in comparison. It is never a sacrifice to serve

Him. It is a privilege to be chosen as His ambassa-
dors. To think that He places such responsibility in
the hands of imperfect men and women, such as you
and I, is an awesome thought. We, who are God's
people, have been chosen *"for such a time as this."*
How can we do less than love Him and serve Him?

When Isaac questioned his father, *"Where is the
lamb?"* (Verse 7), Abraham answered prophetically,
"God will provide himself a lamb." He was speaking by
the inspiration of the Spirit of God and indicating
that God would one day send His Son to be the perfect sacrifice for sins, the Lamb whose death would
result in redemption for all mankind.

God knows what He is doing. His way is best.
Trust Him and you will have victory in your own
personal life and will become a blessing to all those
around you.   📖

- 2 -

LEARN TO HEAR THE VOICE OF GOD

And there was a famine in the land, beside the first famine that was in the days of Abraham. And Isaac went unto Abimelech king of the Philistines unto Gerar. And the Lord appeared unto him, and said, Go not down into Egypt; dwell in the land which I shall tell thee of: Sojourn in this land, and I will be with thee, and will bless thee; for unto thee, and unto thy seed, I will give all these countries, and I will perform the oath which I sware unto Abraham thy father; And I will make thy seed to multiply as the stars of heaven, and will give unto thy seed all these countries; and in thy seed shall all the nations of the earth be blessed; Because that Abraham obeyed my voice, and kept my charge, my com-

mandments, my statutes, and my laws. And
Isaac dwelt in Gerar: Genesis 26:1-6

Ginny and I have ministered in nations that experience frequent famines — among them: various nations of Africa and the Indian subcontinent — and we can witness to the fact that famine is not a pretty thing. Those who go through it seldom forget the experience.

Abraham also knew what it was to face famine. He and Sarah were forced to flee to Egypt for safety, as Jacob's sons would in the time of Joseph's glory. As Isaac was growing up, he probably heard his parents speak frequently of that difficult time of their life. Abraham, no doubt, tried to prepare Isaac for the hard times that he was almost sure to encounter along life's way. And it happened just as his father had said it would.

No rain had fallen for a long time, and when Isaac looked closely at the soil of Canaan, he noticed that it was so dry it was turning to dust. The plants were long since scorched and nothing was growing. How was he to feed his family? He must act quickly.

Fortunately, Isaac remembered what his father had taught him and knew immediately what he must do. Calling his family together, he advised them that they would have to move out quickly toward Egypt and that they should gather up the essential things for their journey.

Before the family got very far, however, God appeared to Isaac and said to him, *"Go not down into Egypt; dwell in the land ... ."*

This was a very critical moment in Isaac's life. As with any good father, he was anxious about how to feed his family. He could not forget the hardships his parents had faced in the first famine, and he desperately wanted to do the right thing. His mind must have been saying, *Get out of here quickly, while there is time.* But the Lord was saying something entirely different.

Isaac was raised to be respectful to his parents and to learn from them, but he was also raised to know the voice of God, who had appeared to his father, Abraham, on ten different occasions. He had learned from his father that God's ways were always right.

If this was God, he must be obedient, but how could he know for sure? I can imagine that any of us might have experienced quite a bit of indecision, if we were placed in Isaac's position.

Once Isaac was sure that he was hearing the voice of God, he did not question or hesitate. He obeyed, although he could not have understood why God was telling him to stay, when He had instructed his father to go.

What God was teaching Isaac through this experience was an important principle. Never base your decisions solely on what has worked for someone else. What brought success to others will not necessarily produce the same results in your life.

Before making major decisions in life, each of us must seek God's direction, without which we can very easily make a wrong, and potentially tragic, move. We cannot afford to make decisions based on our own understanding. We are too limited in this regard and such decisions can produce tragedy.

The Lord told Isaac that if he would stay where he was, He would give him victory over his enemies and would fulfill the oath He had made to his father and repeated that promise to Isaac.

> *I will make thy seed to multiply as the stars of heaven, and will give unto thy seed all these countries; and in thy seed shall all the nations of the earth be blessed;*

These promised blessings were a result, the Lord said, of the obedience of Abraham:

> *Because that Abraham obeyed my voice, and kept my charge, my commandments, my statutes, and my laws.*

What a powerful testimony! No wonder Abraham's children were blessed!

If you are being persecuted by your family for your faith in God, take courage. You are doing the right thing. You have made the right decision. Your loved ones may not understand you now, but one day they will realize that your decision to love and obey God has brought blessing upon the entire family.

What was the decision of Isaac, in the face of this knowledge?

> *And Isaac dwelt in Gerar:*

And what was the result of Isaac's obedience?

Then Isaac sowed in that land, and received in the same year an hundredfold: and the Lord blessed him. Genesis 26:12

That should be an encouragement to every one of us. Obedience pays vast dividends. It is wise to do what pleases God. You cannot lose by hearkening to His voice. I challenge you to be faithful to obey the voice of the Almighty, and I promise you that you will reap endless rewards.

But Isaac had to sow in the time of famine. That required faith on his part, for the land was dry and parched and did not appear to be capable of producing a crop.

But, whatever the circumstances, we must plant. We must plant by faith; for it is impossible to reap if we don't sow. We can only reap in the measure we sow. If we sow bountifully, we will reap bountifully. If we sow sparingly, we will also reap sparingly.

It was the obedience of Isaac that produced his miracle. He refused to look at the circumstances or to listen to the discouraging words of his neighbors. He held in his heart the words of God and clung to them until victory came. The result was a great harvest.

In a short period of time, Isaac became prosperous — to the point of causing envy among his neighbors.

And the man waxed great, and went forward, and grew until he became very great: For he had

possession of flocks, and possession of herds, and
great store of servants: and the Philistines en-
vied him.   Genesis 26:13-14

People may envy you when you are blessed of the
Lord, but don't let that stop you. Be faithful to God in
your own way, and let other people answer to God
for themselves. If some people wrongfully treat you,
pray for them, as Jesus taught.

But I say unto you, Love your enemies, bless
them that curse you, do good to them that hate
you, and pray for them which despitefully use
you, and persecute you;   Matthew 5:44

When the servants of Isaac dug a well to supply
water for their families and their flocks, the Philistines would come along and fill the well up with dirt
and rocks. Isaac refused to strive with them, however, preferring to move on to another place than to
have hard feelings with his neighbors.

But the envy of other men followed him. When his
servants dug a needed well in their new home, the
men of that place came along and claimed it as their
own. Rather than strive with them, Isaac ordered his
servants to let them have it and to dig another.

The same thing happened a second time. This time
Isaac took his family and moved further and dug still
another well. And when he did this, God brought
peace and prosperity to his household.

And he removed from thence, and digged another well; and for that they strove not: and he called the name of it Rehoboth; and he said, For now the Lord hath made room for us, and we shall be fruitful in the land. Genesis 26:22

Peace sometimes comes at a price; but we can have peace if we are willing to do whatever is necessary to avoid strife. Every one of us needs to make a determination to avoid strife within the home and within the work place. This would be a much more pleasant world if each of us did not constantly insist on having things his or her own way.

It is not always necessary to have things go your way and to insist on your point of view. And always remember, you gain nothing by putting someone else down, by making someone else look bad, or by embarrassing someone else or making them feel ashamed.

Jesus said:

Blessed are the peacemakers: for they shall be called the children of God. Matthew 5:9

Being a peacemaker is a worthy goal for which each of us should strive every day.

When Isaac determined to be kind and loving to those around him, despite the desire of others to take advantage of him, God *"made room"* for him and made him *"fruitful in the land."*

Not long after this, God led Isaac to Beersheba and appeared to him there.

> *And he went up from thence to Beersheba. And the Lord appeared unto him the same night, and said, I am the God of Abraham thy father: fear not, for I am with thee, and will bless thee, and multiply thy seed for my servant Abraham's sake. And he builded an altar there, and called upon the name of the Lord, and pitched his tent there: and there Isaac's servants digged a well.*
>
> Genesis 26:23-25

God has made room for you too. He has no quotas. He has declared that whoever will come to His water may drink and that there is an abundant supply.

> *Ho, every one that thirsteth, come ye to the waters, and he that hath no money; come ye, buy, and eat; yea, come, buy wine and milk without money and without price.*   Isaiah 55:1

Are you facing a period of famine in your life? Don't panic. God is still God. He has never changed. He can make room for you and cause you to be fruitful in the land. He can make you a tree of righteousness and load your branches with love, joy, peace, long suffering, gentleness, goodness, faith, meekness, and temperance.

And He will do it today, if you learn to hear His voice and obey His commands.   📖

- 3 -

LEARN TO FIGHT FEAR WITH FAITH

And Elijah the Tishbite, who was of the inhabit-
ants of Gilead, said unto Ahab, As the Lord God
of Israel liveth, before whom I stand, there shall
not be dew nor rain these years, but according to
my word.   1 Kings 17:1

Few individuals in the Bible accomplished more in life or displayed more of the power of God than Elijah. As we can see here, he spoke with great power and authority. What is remarkable about these words is that they were not spoken to just any common citizen of Israel, but to King Ahab, a greatly respected and feared man.

Soon after Elijah had made this declaration, God sent him to live beside the Cherith brook, where He miraculously supplied the prophet's needs — while the nation suffered through a long drought. Every day, at mealtime, ravens were sent to bring food to God's man, and he drank from the brook. He never suffered lack during those difficult days.

But, as the drought which Elijah had so correctly prophesied worsened, the water of the brook began to dry up, too. And one day he found that his source of life-sustaining water had been taken from him.

In his moment of desperation, God spoke to Elijah to go to a place called Zarephath and present himself to a widow who lived there. She would, God promised, sustain him.

How humbling it must have been for this great prophet to have to rely on a poor widow who could hardly take care of her own needs, let alone the needs of others! Sometimes the Lord has to bring us very low so that we understand that all power and supply belongs to Him and that He provides our needs in the manner pleasing to Him — which is usually not the way we would choose.

But Elijah had no choice. He was desperate. So he went to Zarephath and met the widow that God had told him about. He must have been surprised to find that she was not a wealthy widow, looking for outlets for her philanthropy, but a desperately poor person responsible for a son, left to her care.

Elijah hated to take anything from this woman. Who wouldn't? But God had shown him that she would fulfill his needs. At last he got up his nerve to ask for a drink of water (no small thing in time of drought).

> *Fetch me, I pray thee, a little water in a vessel,*
> *that I may drink.*   1 Kings 17:10

Hunger overcame his pride, and as she was going for the water, Elijah called to the widow and asked if she had anything to eat, even a *"morsel of bread"* (Verse 11).

The women replied that she had no bread at all and that all she did have was a *"handful of meal in a barrel and a little oil in a cruse."* She went on to describe her plight:

> *And, behold, I am gathering two sticks, that I*
> *may go in and dress it for me and my son, that*
> *we may eat it, and die.*   1 Kings 17:12

What a desperate situation! How could Elijah accept anything at all from this woman? She was much worse off than he was. And here he was asking her to give him something — when she had so little for herself. But as Elijah contemplated why God would have sent him to a woman in such desperation, the anointing of the Lord came upon him, and he began to prophesy:

> *Fear not; go and do as thou hast said: but make*
> *me thereof a little cake first, and bring it unto*
> *me, and after make for thee and for thy son.*
>   1 Kings 17:13

The widow offered no objection and proceeded to do exactly what the prophet had spoken. When she had finished preparing for the man of God, she returned to the barrel, and found that it was not empty (as it had been when she last looked inside) and to the cruse and found that it was not empty either (as it too had been). This is exactly what Elijah had prophesied would happen:

> *For thus saith the Lord God of Israel, The barrel*
> *of meal shall not waste, neither shall the cruse of*
> *oil fail, until the day that the Lord sendeth rain*
> *upon the earth.*   1 Kings 17:14

This was not a onetime miracle. It happened day after day, and week after week, until the famine had run its course.

> *She, and he [Elijah], and her house, did eat many*
> *days. And the barrel of meal wasted not, neither*
> *did the cruse of oil fail, according to the word of*
> *the Lord, which he spake by Elijah.*
>   1 Kings 17:15-16

What a wonderful miracle!

After a time the woman's son became ill and died. In her grief, she turned on the prophet and accused him of causing her son's death. Good friends can quickly turn into fierce enemies when troubles come to their lives. Don't be surprised when it happens. Elijah took the child and carried him to the loft where he himself slept, placed him on his own bed, and began to pray.

The prophet was perplexed by what had happened. He was frustrated by the brook drying up, by being forced into this uncomfortable position and now by having the widow, his benefactor, turning against him. In his frustration, he blamed God for what had happened.

> *And he cried unto the Lord, and said, O Lord my God, hast thou also brought evil upon the widow with whom I sojourn, by slaying her son?*
> 1 Kings 17:20

As he prayed, Elijah was reminded that God loves us and that everything that God does is for our benefit. He is never to be blamed for the adversities we may face in life. We must first ask ourselves if something we have done has placed us in the position in which we find ourselves and not be so quick to blame someone else.

Secondly, we must ask ourselves what God is trying to do in our lives. What is He trying to teach us?

And, thirdly, we must call out to God to deliver us and to glorify His name in our circumstances. As he prayed, God showed Elijah what to do to bring the child back to life.

> *And he stretched himself upon the child three times, and cried unto the Lord, and said, O Lord my God, I pray thee, let this child's soul come into him again. And the Lord heard the voice of Elijah; and the soul of the child came into him*

*again, and he revived. And Elijah took the child,
and brought him down out of the chamber into
the house, and delivered him unto his mother:
and Elijah said, See, thy son liveth.*

1 Kings 17:21-23

The widow was deeply moved by this demonstration of God's power through the prophet.

*And the woman said to Elijah, Now by this I
know that thou art a man of God, and that the
word of the Lord in thy mouth is truth.*

1 Kings 17:24

Actions always speak louder than words. People are far more impressed with a demonstration of God's power, a miracle, than they are with what we say. But this woman had already seen God's power at work. Her meal had been multiplied every day. Her oil had been multiplied every day. She and her son had been saved from starvation by the miracles of God. How quick we are to forget His goodness! May the Lord help us to be ever mindful of His love and to never accuse Him when we suffer pain and trouble.

The next great event in the life of Elijah was the contest of good vs. evil with the four hundred and fifty prophets of Baal. He proposed the contest himself and did it publicly, in the presence of a great crowd of people, because those people had been seduced by the false prophets.

So Ahab sent unto all the children of Israel, and gathered the prophets together unto mount Carmel. And Elijah came unto all the people, and said, How long halt ye between two opinions? if the Lord be God, follow him: but if Baal, then follow him. And the people answered him not a word. Then said Elijah unto the people, I, even I only, remain a prophet of the Lord; but Baal's prophets are four hundred and fifty men. Let them therefore give us two bullocks; and let them choose one bullock for themselves, and cut it in pieces, and lay it on wood, and put no fire under: and I will dress the other bullock, and lay it on wood, and put no fire under: And call ye on the name of your gods, and I will call on the name of the Lord: and the God that answereth by fire, let him be God. And all the people answered and said, it is well spoken.   1 Kings 18:20-24

The people had not entirely abandoned Jehovah, but were convinced that Baal also had power. So, they were trying to serve both gods. *"How long will you be between two opinions,"* Elijah demanded and proposed the demonstration which would show, once and for all, which god had power. He gave the prophets of Baal the first opportunity.

And Elijah said unto the prophets of Baal, Choose you one bullock for yourselves, and dress it first; for ye are many; and call on the name of your gods, but put no fire under. And they took

*the bullock which was given them, and they
dressed it, and called on the name of Baal from
morning even until noon, saying, O Baal, hear
us. But there was no voice, nor any that answered. And they leaped upon the altar which
was made.*   1 Kings 18:25-26

When nothing happened, Elijah mocked the false
prophets, and they, fearing public humiliation, ex-
erted themselves even more, in an effort to produce
some sort of miracle.

*And they cried aloud, and cut themselves after
their manner with knives and lancets, till the
blood gushed out upon them. And it came to
pass, when midday was past, and they prophesied until the time of the offering of the evening
sacrifice, that there was neither voice, nor any to
answer, nor any that regarded.*
1 Kings 18:28-29

Having humiliated the false prophets, Elijah proceeded to prove the power of the Living God.

*And Elijah said unto all the people, Come near
unto me. And all the people came near unto him.
And he repaired the altar of the Lord that was
broken down. And Elijah took twelve stones, according to the number of the tribes of the sons of
Jacob, unto whom the word of the Lord came,*

saying, Israel shall be thy name: And with the stones he built an altar in the name of the Lord: and he made a trench about the altar, as great as would contain two measures of seed. And he put the wood in order, and cut the bullock in pieces, and laid him on the wood, and said, Fill four barrels with water, and pour it on the burnt sacrifice, and on the wood.

And he said, Do it the second time. And they did it the second time.

And he said, Do it the third time. And they did it the third time. And the water ran round about the altar; and he filled the trench also with water.

And it came to pass at the time of the offering of the evening sacrifice, that Elijah the prophet came near, and said, Lord God of Abraham, Isaac, and of Israel, let it be known this day that thou art God in Israel, and that I am thy servant, and that I have done all these things at thy word. Hear me, O Lord, hear me, that this people may know that thou art the Lord God, and that thou hast turned their heart back again.

Then the fire of the Lord fell, and consumed the burnt sacrifice, and the wood, and the stones, and the dust, and licked up the water that was in the trench. And when all the people saw it, they fell on their faces: and they said, The Lord, he is the God; the Lord, he is the God.

1 Kings 18:30-39

Despite the fact that twelve barrels of water had been poured over the sacrifice, it was immediately consumed by fire. No wonder it brought such a response from the people.

Afterward, Elijah commanded that the prophets of Baal be destroyed, and, to make sure that his command was carried out, he helped the people do what was necessary.

> *And Elijah said unto them, Take the prophets of*
> *Baal; let not one of them escape. And they took*
> *them: and Elijah brought* them down to the
> brook Kishon, and slew them there.
>
> *1 Kings 18:40*

Soon God showed Elijah that it was time to end the drought and sent him to speak with King Ahab and tell him to prepare for rain. This is something that all of us need to do. The sun may be shining today, but it will surely rain again. Troubles will surely come our way. We must be ready for anything and everything that tomorrow may bring. Whatever happens tomorrow, we must each be found living a life pleasing to God, a life of prayer and praise, fasting, Bible study and good works toward others. If we are prepared, we can weather any storm. If the Lord is in the ship with us, we will always be safe.

The king believed Elijah and got in his chariot and raced toward Jezreel, but the power of God was upon the prophet and he outran the chariot.

When word reached the pagan Queen Jezebel that Elijah had challenged the four hundred and fifty prophets of Baal to a test, had publicly humiliated them and had them slain, that he had prophesied the end of the drought and had outrun the kings's chariot to Jezreel, she was furious and determined to kill Elijah. And she didn't waste any time telling him what she was going to do to him.

> *Then Jezebel sent a messenger unto Elijah, saying, So let the gods do to me, and more also, if I make not thy life as the life of one of them by to morrow about this time.*   1 Kings 19:2

Would Elijah be intimidated by this? Surely not. He was a man of power, a man of the prophetic word. What he spoke came to pass. When he said it would not rain for several years, the heavens were shut and it did not rain. When he said there would be ample food for the widow, her son and himself, there was enough. When he spoke words of life to the dead boy, he was resurrected from the dead. When he called fire down from heaven, it consumed the soaked sacrifice and even lapped up the dust around the trench. Shortly after he advised Ahab that it would soon rain again, the sky darkened and the rains began to fall. What did he have to fear?

If he could call fire from heaven and command that the prophets of Baal be slain, surely he would not be intimidated by a pagan woman. He could easily have called wolves to come out of the forest to destroy her, command her to be dumb and never to speak again, or send for a legion of angels to come to his assistance. But he did none of these things. HE RAN FOR HIS LIFE IN FEAR OF JEZEBEL.

> *And when he saw that, he arose, and went for his life, and came to Beersheba, which belongeth to Judah, and left his servant there. But he himself went a day's journey into the wilderness, and came and sat down under a juniper tree: and he requested for himself that he might die; and said, it is enough; now, O Lord, take away my life; for I am not better than my fathers.*
>
> 1 Kings 19:3-4

Some have made much of the fact that Elijah ran from a woman. I think that is not the point. This was not just any woman. This woman was very powerful and influential. The point is that Elijah, who had faced so many trials bravely, now ran from his trouble. He forgot, for a moment, who he was. He forgot, for a moment, that His God was greater than any trouble. The fear which Jezebel's words invoked caused him to act irrationally. He not only ran, but he ran a day's journey before he ever stopped.

The fact that he hid under a juniper tree is meaningful to me because we had junipers in our front yard when we lived in Maryland. Two things come to mind about those junipers. They were very low to the ground, and they were full of stickers. To get under a juniper tree you would have to sink very low. And you would almost certainly be scratched in the process.

Fear is a paralyzing force that causes us to do irrational things. Elijah was even praying to die. What a sad turn of events! If he had really wanted to die, why didn't he stay and face Jezebel? If he had really wanted to die, why did he run *"a day's journey"* before he stopped? If he really wanted to die, why was he hiding under a juniper tree?

How significant it is that God did not abandon the prophet in his hour of sadness! An angel was sent to minister to Elijah.

After he was there for a while, the angel came and ministered to him a second time, this time giving him food that gave him supernatural strength.

Now, Elijah sought out a cave and hid there. It was in the cave that God spoke to him again.

> *What doest thou here, Elijah?*   1 Kings 19:9

With so much to be done, what was such a mighty and useful man doing hiding in an isolated cave? Elijah's answer is interesting.

> *And he said, I have been very jealous for the Lord God of hosts: for the children of Israel have forsaken thy covenant, thrown down thine altars, and slain thy prophets with the sword; and I, even I only, am left; and they seek my life, to take it away.*   1 Kings 19:10

Surely each of us can identify somewhat with Elijah's words. There are times when each of us feels all alone: all alone, fighting against multiple enemies; all alone, keeping the faith. Elijah fully believed that he was alone and insisted on it the second time.

> *And he said, I have been very jealous for the Lord God of hosts: because the children of Israel have forsaken thy covenant, thrown down thine altars, and slain thy prophets with the sword; and I, even I only, am left; and they seek my life, to take it away.*   1 Kings 19:14

But God's question to Elijah did not change.

> *Elijah ... wrapped his face in his mantle, and went out, and stood in the entering in of the cave. And, behold, there came a voice unto him, and said, What doest thou here, Elijah?*
> 1 Kings 19:13

This is not the time to sit in solitude and ponder the whys of life. People are dying without Christ. They are desperate for the truth. Thousands need deliverance and healing. This is not the time to be hiding in a cave.

Besides that, we are NOT alone, and neither was Elijah, and God told him so.

> *Yet I have left me seven thousand in Israel, all the knees which have not bowed unto Baal, and every mouth which hath not kissed him.*
> 1 Kings 19:18

While Elijah felt all alone, God had another seven thousand dependable people who loved Him. He always has His people, even in the most unlikely places. We are not alone.

Elijah's life was nearing its end, and God had one last assignment for him: to anoint Hazael king over Syria, Jehu king over Israel and Elisha to take the prophet's place. There is no further record concerning the command to anoint Hazael and Jehu, but Elijah did train Elisha to take his place and, thus, ensured succession.

Apparently, Elijah's ministry was ended prematurely by his fear of Jezebel, by his running from his trouble, by his putting too much emphasis on what he had done for God and by his not being sufficiently conscious of the fact that God had given him all the abilities he possessed. Let us be among those who give all the glory to Jesus.

Learn to overcome fear with faith, for fear is a deadly force, which, if left unchecked, will destroy your life. 📖

- 4 -

LEARN TO BE STUBBORN IN YOUR RESOLVE

So he departed thence, and found Elisha the son of Shaphat, who was plowing with twelve yoke of oxen before him, and he with the twelfth: and Elijah passed by him, and cast his mantle upon him. And he left the oxen, and ran after Elijah, and said, Let me, I pray thee, kiss my father and my mother, and then I will follow thee. And he said unto him, Go back again: for what have I done to thee? And he returned back from him, and took a yoke of oxen, and slew them, and boiled their flesh with the instruments of the oxen, and gave unto the people, and they did eat. Then he arose, and went after Elijah, and minis-tered unto him.   1 Kings 19:19-21

I cannot believe that this was the first time Elisha had thought of leaving his oxen and following God. I am sure that he had been pondering this decision for a long time. Now, when Elijah cast the mantle over him, he realized that it was time to obey God and acted quickly.

Elisha did several important things: he went back to pay his respects once more to his family and to inform them of his decision. Then he burned his bridges behind him, destroying the oxen that provided his income and using them as part of the farewell feast. He was now dependent upon the Lord, and he never looked back, but set out to follow Elijah and to minister to him. There is no better way to learn the ways of God than from a faithful servant of God. To Elisha, leaving all to follow the Lord was not a sacrifice, and he entered into his new life with great enthusiasm.

To many of us who are called to serve the Lord, this seems like a very difficult time. These are life and death decisions. How can we be sure that we will be successful in the ministry? How can we be sure that the Lord will provide our needs? The first way we know is His faithfulness to His promises. His Word declares:

> *But my God shall supply all your need according to his riches in glory by Christ Jesus.*
> Philippians 4:19

When we are just starting out, however, we have not proven His promises. All we know is that we are accustomed to working to support ourselves. If we don't work, we don't eat. That is a general rule of life. It has never been necessary to trust someone else to supply those needs. And can we trust someone else to do it?

If we have done well in secular life, sometimes the decision is even harder. Because we have done well in taking care of family and business matters, it is not an easy thing to now blindly turn this responsibility over to someone else. Will another person understand our needs as we understand them? Could another person feel the same responsibility we feel with regard to our own spouse and children?

But, when you think about it, if we are accepting a call from God, we are entrusting our future and that of our family to Him, not to any man. That makes all the difference in the world.

When Ginny and I decided to take this step, leaving our secular income to enter the ministry full time, our faith for finances was still very small. Because of that, God allowed a couple — who just happened to be about our same age and our same social level — to come into our lives. They, too, had been very successful in the business world and had provided for themselves a very good living. Then, they told us, God directed them to leave it all and follow Him to the mission field — while they still had several small children.

The testimony of that couple really challenged us, and we reasoned that if God could provide for their family, He certainly could do the same for us. So, we prepared to take the plunge.

In a very short time, therefore, God wrapped up all the loose ends for us, as He had for Elisha. His oxen were so valuable, and he didn't want to be tempted to return to them when things might get rough, so he just ate them and shared them with his neighbors. What great wisdom that was!

> *And it came to pass, when the Lord would take up Elijah into heaven by a whirlwind, that Elijah went with Elisha from Gilgal.*
>
> 2 Kings 2:1

With these opening words of the second book of Kings, Elisha's training intensified. God was about to take his master home, and everything that Elisha had learned must soon be put to the test. And there were some very important last-minute lessons that he must digest, as well.

Elisha determined to stay close to the prophet during the final moments of his life on earth. Stepping into these shoes was a big order, and he must learn all he could while there was time.

Elijah wanted to go to Bethel one last time. "You can stay here if you want," he told Elisha. But Elisha could not agree:

> *And Elisha said unto him, As the Lord liveth, and as thy soul liveth, I will not leave thee. So they went down to Bethel.*   2 Kings 2:2

Elisha was determined not to stand still, not to look back. He had to keep moving forward. He would not be left behind. He wanted to be where God was moving. He wanted to be where the action was.

When they reached Bethel, the *"sons of the prophets"* were waiting there. You would think they would want to encourage the young trainee, but not so. They whispered to him, as if this were some game:

> *Knowest thou that the Lord will take away thy master from thy head to day?* 2 Kings 2:3

Elisha replied that he knew what was about to take place but that he didn't want to discuss it. It was not a time to be distracted. He had serious business to attend to.

Elijah decided to go on to Jericho and suggested that Elisha stay behind. Elisha again declined, insisting on staying close to his master.

> *And he said, As the Lord liveth, and as thy soul liveth, I will not leave thee. So they came to Jericho.* 2 Kings 2:4

This may be the only context where the word "stubborn" can be applied in a favorable light. Elisha was stubborn, determined, relentless.

The same scene that took place with the sons of the prophets at Bethel was repeated at Jericho. We all encounter people along our pathway in life who try to get us sidetracked so that we will miss out on

God's best arrangement for us. We need to be single-minded in dealing with these people, as was Elisha. Keep your eye on the goal. Elisha again refused to be distracted by speculation and idle conversation. He had work to do.

Now, Elijah felt compelled to go to the Jordan. He again suggested that Elisha might like to stay behind and wait for him. This time Elisha must have been tempted to obey. They had done a lot of traveling for one day, and he was very tired, very hot, and very dusty from the trail. He had never been this far from home before. A good rest might restore his flagging spirits.

But, no, he could not stay behind. His answer was exactly the same this time as it had been before. Tiredness had not changed his response. Weariness had not moved him to retreat.

> *And he said, As the Lord liveth, and as thy soul liveth, I will not leave thee. And they two went on.*   2 Kings 2:6

Fifty sons of the prophets followed them to the Jordan but stood back at a distance to watch what was about to take place. Elisha would not have been satisfied to stand back and watch. He wanted to be in the middle of things, experiencing and learning.

It is easy to stand back and watch what others are doing. Those who do this have wonderful criticisms. The strange thing is that they never do anything themselves. They can only criticize what others do.

We desperately need fewer spectators and more participants in the Kingdom of God.

When the two men reached the Jordan, a wonderful miracle took place.

> *And Elijah took his mantle, and wrapped it together, and smote the waters, and they were divided hither and thither, so that they two went over on dry ground.* 2 Kings 2:8

This was the same miracle that Moses had witnessed at the Red Sea and that Joshua had witnessed at the Jordan when he first crossed over to possess the land. God had not changed, Elisha could see. He was still performing miracles for His people.

And, with the miraculous crossing of the Jordan, the final scene of this great drama begins to unfold, the moment of truth, as it were. As if out of the blue, the old prophet turns to the young replacement and asks, "What can I do for you?"

> *And it came to pass, when they were gone over, that Elijah said unto Elisha, Ask what I shall do for thee, before I be taken away from thee.* 2 Kings 2:9

The question must have been on the mind of Elisha ever since they began their journey. No doubt the devil had been tormenting him all along the way, by saying:

> *Who do you think you are, seeking such great*
> *power from God. You are so full of pride that*
> *God would never be able to use you. You haven't*
> *done anything, and you will never be an Elijah.*
> *You might as well go on home and get yourself a*
> *good team of oxen again. You surely are not*
> *ready to take over this man's ministry.*

I wasn't there and these words are not recorded in the Bible, but this is exactly the way Satan tries to batter any man or woman who dares to accept the call of God to work for Him.

But Elisha was not shaken.

> *And Elisha said, I pray thee, let a double portion*
> *of thy spirit be upon me.*   2 Kings 2:9

Elisha knew that God had called him, and if God had called him, God knew that he *could* do the job. He would not let anything discourage him. He would press on to a double portion.

There! He had said it! And he waited for the reply.

The old prophet looked at the young man and said, "Son, you've asked a hard thing."

Perhaps the young man's spirit wavered for a moment, and perhaps the devil murmured in his ear:

> *See! What did I tell you? You're young. You're*
> *a novice. You haven't even faced a real test. And*
> *here you are asking for a double portion. What a*
> *proud one you are.*

If it happened that way, Elisha, as before, pushed these thoughts from his mind. He was single-minded. He would not be denied. He would not listen to the devil. He stood his ground and waited for Elijah to finish his statement.

> *And he said, Thou hast asked a hard thing: nevertheless, if thou see me when I am taken from thee, it shall be so unto thee; but if not, it shall not be so.*   2 Kings 2:10

Elisha must have been rejoicing when he heard those words. He had faced the test and would receive the reward. Nothing would stop him now.

It is not wrong to expect great things from God, and if you have proper motives (that is: you want to use God's gifts for the advancement of His Kingdom), there is no limit to what you can ask of God. It is not prideful to think big. Faith demands that you do it.

The two men were walking on, talking as they went, when, suddenly, the whole area was filled with the power and the glory of God. It appeared as fire and filled the air around them. A great *"chariot of fire"* swooped down and parted the two men. Then Elijah was swept up by a *"whirlwind"* into the very presence of God.

Thus, ended the ministry of one man; and, thus, began the ministry of another. The fire of God is a wonderful thing. It purifies us and prepares us for the ministry that is ahead.

If God is calling you to work for Him, don't resist
His preparation. If it takes the form of fiery trials,
rejoice because through those trials God is working
out His purpose in your life.

> *And he saw him no more: and he took hold of his*
> *own clothes, and rent them in two pieces.*
>
> 2 Kings 2:12

When all the dust had settled, when the chariot of
fire had vanished, along with the horses of fire, when
the eddies caused by the whirlwind had died down,
there must have been a deadly silence. And this was
the greatest hour of Elisha's test. He was alone now.
He was still looking up, but *"he saw him [Elijah] no
more."* That made it final. He was on his own now.
He would have to prove that God was with him and
that he could, indeed, fill Elijah's shoes.

In that moment, he took hold of his garments and
tore them. His clothes were a reminder of his carnal
self. It must not be allowed to hinder what God
wanted to do in him and through him. He ripped
them, putting off all the old ways, the natural con-
nections, and he now took up the mantle of God's
power and authority to continue the work of the
Lord.

> *He took up also the mantle of Elijah that fell*
> *from him, and went back, and stood by the bank*
> *of Jordan; And he took the mantle of Elijah that*
> *fell from him, and smote the waters, and said,*

Where is the Lord God of Elijah? and when he also had smitten the waters, they parted hither and thither: and Elisha went over.

2 Kings 2:13-14

When Elisha smote the waters in the same way that Elijah had done, they parted for him, just as they had for Elijah. The reaction of the sons of the prophets shows us what this act did for Elisha as a spiritual leader.

And when the sons of the prophets which were to view at Jericho saw him, they said, The spirit of Elijah doth rest on Elisha. And they came to meet him, and bowed themselves to the ground before him.   2 Kings 2:15

They had been waiting to see what would happen. Now, they got an eye full. *"The spirit of Elijah rests on Elisha."* What more could they say?

When you take up the mantle God has given you and begin to do the things He has called you to do, you will elicit the same response from others.

The Lord is looking for those who are willing to be trained for the ministry and to *"about the Father's business."* Will you be one of those? And will you demonstrate a stubborn determination to be true to your decision?   📖

- 5 -

LEARNING TO PRACTICE WHAT YOU PREACH

Now Elisha was fallen sick of his sickness whereof he died.   2 Kings 13:14

The double portion prophet, it seems, was not able to complete his ministry, but died prematurely of a serious sickness. The circumstances of his death were unusual: Elisha was lying on his bed in his last extremity, gasping for breath, when King Joash came into the chamber. He was not coming to comfort the prophet, but to say that the Syrians were coming against him, and he didn't know what to do about it. Poor Elisha couldn't even die in peace. He had to forget his own problems for the moment and try to help the king.

Elisha told the king to take a bow and arrow, and with his hand and the king's hand on the bow, the king was to open the window and shoot the arrow eastward. The prophet called this shot *"the arrow of the Lord's deliverance."* Then Elisha told the king to smite the ground with his arrows. When the king struck the ground three times and stopped, Elisha was angry. The king should have struck the ground five or six times, he said, not just three times. In other words, he gave up too soon or too easily. Now, the prophet warned, his victory against the Syrians would not be complete.

As I read this portion of scripture, I have to wonder why the prophet did not listen to his own sermon, why he did not take his own advice. If it was good for the king, it was good for the prophet, as well.

If I understand this passage correctly, it appears to me that Elisha also gave up too soon. He was destined for greater things. If Elijah escaped death and went to glory in a whirlwind, and if Elisha was promised a double portion of all that Elijah had experienced, surely his passing should have been a glorious one.

There can be no doubt that the sickness Elisha suffered was a serious one, but this was no reason to lay down and die. His work was not yet finished. He had no right to quit. Only God can decide when our time has come.

Elisha died and was buried; but, after his death, the Bible records a very interesting occurrence.

A band of invading robbers, Moabites, came into the cemetery to bury one of their own. While they were in the process of burying their friend, they were disturbed to see a band of local people approaching. They dispensed with the niceties and tossed the dead body into the nearest sepulchre. That just happened to be the tomb of Elisha, and when the body of their friend touched the bones of the prophet, he got a touch of the glory that had been upon the man of God, and he came to life again.

> *And it came to pass, as they were burying a man, that, behold, they spied a band of men; and they cast the man into the sepulchre of Elisha: and when the man was let down, and touched the bones of Elisha, he revived, and stood up on his feet.* 2 Kings 13:21

Nothing more is recorded of the incident, but this is enough to show us that there was enough power left in the bones of the dead prophet to put life back in a dead man. And, if that was true, there certainly must have been enough power in the prophet to keep himself alive, to get deliverance from the sickness that cut his life short.

He told the king, "Joash, you gave up too soon."

And I want to tell the prophet, "Elisha, you gave up too soon, also."

And I want to tell every servant of God:

LEARN TO PRACTICE WHAT YOU PREACH!

Our strength is certainly limited, but His is unlimited. When we feel that there is no more strength in us and that we must faint along the way, we can tap into His strength and get up and go forward again.

If a great prophet of God like Elisha could be sidelined before his work was completed, it can happen to any one of us. We must be single-minded and have a dogged determination not to allow any trick of the enemy to divert our attention from the goal. He will not rest from his attempts to hinder and discourage us, so we must not rest from our determination to continue on faithfully until the job is finished. God's strength is sufficient for that which He has called us to do. Onward, soldiers of the cross. Let us complete the work, by learning to practice what we preach.

- 6 -

LEARN TO PUT THE NATURAL MAN IN HIS PLACE

*Then the king of Syria warred against Israel,
and took counsel with his servants, saying, In
such and such a place shall be my camp.*

*And the man of God sent unto the king of Israel,
saying, Beware that thou pass not such a place;
for thither the Syrians are come down.*

*And the king of Israel sent to the place which the
man of God told him and warned him of, and
saved himself there, not once nor twice.*

*Therefore the heart of the king of Syria was sore
troubled for this thing; and he called his servants, and said unto them, Will ye not shew me
which of us is for the king of Israel?*

*And one of his servants said, None, my lord, O
king: but Elisha, the prophet that is in Israel,*

> *telleth the king of Israel the words that thou*
> *speakest in thy bedchamber.*   2 Kings 6:8-12

This amazing Old Testament story emphasizes a truth that each of us must learn, if we are to be victorious in life. The natural man is limited, and we must learn to put him in his place.

Syria was waging war with Israel, and the King of Syria set ambushes, time and time again, to catch the children of Israel. Each time he set such a trap his plot was somehow made known to his enemies. He finally became convinced that there was a spy in the camp.

When an aide informed him that his plans were being divulged by a "prophet" named Elisha, he took a large contingent of chariots and cavalry and surrounded the prophet's quarters under cover of darkness. When a servant named Gehazi went outside early in the morning, he was startled to see the hillside covered with Syrian troops.

> *And when the servant of the man of God was*
> *risen early, and gone forth, behold, an host com-*
> *passed the city both with horses and chariots.*
> 2 Kings 6:15

Alarmed, Gehazi rushed back inside and told Elisha the troubling news. Elisha, however, had a different reaction to the news than had been expected.

> *And he answered, Fear not: for they that be with*
> *us are more than they that be with them.*
> 2 Kings 6:16

Gehazi must have wondered if his master had taken leave of his senses. He knew what he had seen outside the door. But the prophet had been in the presence of the Lord and knew that despite the circumstances everything was going to be alright.

The difference between the reactions of Gehazi and Elisha to the appearance of enemy troops shows us perfectly the difference between natural man and supernatural man.

This was not the first time the two men had reacted differently:

When Naaman, the Syrian captain, traveled to Israel in search of healing for his leprosy, Elisha told him to *"go and wash seven times"* in the Jordan River (2 Kings 5:10). When Naaman obeyed, he was healed.

> *Then went he down, and dipped himself seven times in Jordan, according to the saying of the man of God: and his flesh came again like unto the flesh of a little child, and he was clean.*
> 2 Kings 5:14

Naaman was an important man in Syria and had brought many gifts with him. He now wanted to reward the prophet, but Elisha refused. He wanted God to have all the glory for what had been done. Gehazi, however, thought it would be a shame to waste the good will of this Syrian, so he decided to take advantage of the situation himself. He followed the entourage of Naaman until he overtook it. Then, he told Naaman that Elisha had changed his mind and would indeed receive his gifts because of some young prophets who had unexpectedly come to visit.

He would do them the favor of carrying everything
back, if they wanted.

Gehazi's wrong was compounded when he lied to
Elisha about where he had been and why he was
returning home with so many treasures.

As a result of Gehazi's attitude, God was angry
with him and struck him with leprosy.

> *The leprosy therefore of Naaman shall cleave
> unto thee, and unto thy seed for ever. And he
> went out from his presence a leper as white as
> snow.*   2 Kings 5:27

What a terrible way for Gehazi to learn his lesson!
Natural man is guided by his senses. When Gehazi
stepped outside the house that morning in Dothan,
he saw a host of enemies surrounding the city. That
meant trouble to him.

A spiritual man is guided by faith and trust in God.
He is moved, not by what he sees or hears, but by
what the Spirit reveals to him. He has faith to believe
that no matter how strong the enemy may be his God
is always stronger. Instead of feeling panic at the
news Gehazi brought, Elisha prayed:

> *Lord, I pray thee, open his eyes, that he may see.*
>   2 Kings 6:17

Gehazi, no doubt, thought he already was seeing
very clearly. He was a "young man" with good eye-
sight. He knew what he had seen. The hillsides were
full of enemy soldiers. What he hadn't seen was that
God was also working in the situation.

So many Christians are like that young man. They can see problems everywhere. They can see every enemy clearly. What they don't see is what God is doing on their behalf. They fail to see His hand in every situation.

This delights the Enemy of our souls. He longs to frighten us, to imprison us in fear, to hinder our faith in God and to drag us down to defeat.

God tells us, in His Word, that any situation we encounter in life, no matter how terrible it may seem at the time, can be turned to our advantage.

> *And we know that all things work together for good to them that love God, to them who are the called according to his purpose.*   Romans 8:28

Elisha knew that Gehazi was not seeing things as they really were. He was blinded by his fear so that he could not see God's hand at work in the situation. He needed to have his eyes opened. When his eyes were opened, he was amazed to see something very different.

> *And the Lord opened the eyes of the young man; and he saw: and, behold, the mountain was full of horses and chariots of fire round about Elisha.*
> 2 Kings 6:17

The very armies of heaven were present on the hillsides of Dothan that morning, and anyone who loved and served God had nothing to fear. If God could reveal to his servant the movements of the enemy king, he could protect him from that king's troops, as well. It was true that the enemy chariots and cavalry divisions had surrounded the city, but it was also true that *"the mountain was full of horses and chariots of fire round about Elisha."* God was at work to deliver His servant.

There are many other examples in scripture of the difference between the natural man and the spiritual man. The natural man strives to fulfil his own lusts and desires, while the spiritual man strives to please God and walk in His ways. The natural man, as a consequence, is blown about by every circumstance of life, while the spiritual man is not influenced at all by circumstances, but overcomes every circumstance of life by the power of God.

The natural man lives in fear, while the spiritual man walks in faith. The natural man is moved by imagination and superstition, often heeding the wrong voices, voices that lead him away from God's will for his life, while the spiritual man is guided by truth and light as he closes his ears to any voice but the voice of God.

We would all do well to pray as Elisha prayed:

> *Lord, open our eyes so that we can see things as they really are. Help us to be sensitive to what You are doing in every situation. Help us to be spiritual and not carnal.*

Let us each learn to put the natural man in his place.   📖

- 7 -

LEARN TO STAY HUMBLE

And I sought for a man among them, that should make up the hedge, and stand in the gap before me for the land, that I should not destroy it: but I found none.   Ezekiel 22:30

What a dark day in history when Father God could not find a single person qualified to *"stand in the gap"* and *"make up the hedge"* to hold back judgment. What kind of person was God looking for?

As I prayed about this one day, the Lord directed me to the book of Daniel.

There is a man in thy kingdom, in whom is the spirit of the holy gods; and in the days of thy father light and understanding and wisdom, like

> *the wisdom of the gods, was found in him; whom*
> *the king Nebuchadnezzar thy father, the king, I*
> *say, thy father, made master of the magicians,*
> *astrologers, Chaldeans, and soothsayers;*
>
> Daniel 5:11

This statement was made by a heathen queen, wife of Belshazzar, King of the Babylonian Empire. She was reminding her husband that Daniel, a Jewish exile brought to Babylon by force under Nebuchadnezzar, Belshazzar's father (or grandfather, historians cannot agree on which), had been able to interpret dreams and dissolve hard sentences during Nebuchadnezzar's reign. In Daniel, she recognized the characteristics that make the type of person that God uses. He had *"light"* and *"understanding"* and *"wisdom."* And she recognized that his wisdom was not worldly wisdom; for she described it as being *"like the wisdom of the gods."*

Daniel was so sensitive to the voice of God that he was able to resolve problems that all the wise men in Babylon could not resolve. Surely he could interpret the handwriting on the wall. *"Let Daniel be called,"* she suggested (Verse 12). Belshazzar agreed, and Daniel was called to appear before him.

"I have heard of thee," the king told Daniel (Verse 14), repeating the phrase again a few moments later:

> *And I have heard of thee, that thou canst make*
> *interpretations, and dissolve doubts: now if thou*
> *canst read the writing, and make known to me*

*the interpretation thereof, thou shalt be clothed
with scarlet, and have a chain of gold about thy
neck, and shalt be the third ruler in the kingdom.*
Daniel 5:16

But Daniel refused the offer. He was not moved by
thoughts of temporal gain, but by the voice of God.
He would, nevertheless, interpret the handwriting,
he assured the king.

*Then Daniel answered and said before the king,
Let thy gifts be to thyself, and give thy rewards
to another; yet I will read the writing unto the
king, and make known to him the interpretation.*
Daniel 5:17

But Daniel would not be rushed. He first had some
other things to say to this king. He reminded him
that God had given Nebuchadnezzar four things.

*O thou king, the most high God gave Nebu-
chadnezzar thy father a kingdom, and majesty,
and glory, and honour:* Daniel 5:18

It was clearly because of God's favor upon him that
Nebuchadnezzar was able to reign effectively.

*And for the majesty that he gave him, all people,
nations, and languages, trembled and feared before him: whom he would he slew; and whom he*

would he kept alive; and whom he would he set
up; and whom he would he put down.

Daniel 5:19

Nebuchadnezzar, as so many men do, failed to recognize that his power was from God, and failed to
give God His due. Instead, he allowed deadly pride
to enter into his heart.

But when his heart was lifted up, and his mind
hardened in pride, he was deposed from his
kingly throne, and they took his glory from him:

Daniel 5:20

Just as his exaltation had come in four steps, the
fall of Nebuchadnezzar came in four steps.

The fall of Nebuchadnezzar was a terrible one. He
became insane and lived with wild animals, being as
one of them.

And he was driven from the sons of men; and his
heart was made like the beasts, and his dwelling
was with the wild asses: they fed him with grass
like oxen, and his body was wet with the dew of
heaven; till he knew that the most high God
ruled in the kingdom of men, and that he
appointeth over it whomsoever he will.

Daniel 5:21

This turn of events should not have come as any
surprise. God had given Nebuchadnezzar a dream, a

dream that troubled him — until Daniel was able to give the interpretation:

> *This is the interpretation, O king, and this is the decree of the most High, which is come upon my lord the king: That they shall drive thee from men, and thy dwelling shall be with the beasts of the field, and they shall make thee to eat grass as oxen, and they shall wet thee with the dew of heaven, and seven times shall pass over thee, till thou know that the most High ruleth in the kingdom of men, and giveth it to whomsoever he will. And whereas they commanded to leave the stump of the tree roots; thy kingdom shall be sure unto thee, after that thou shalt have known that the heavens do rule. Wherefore, O king, let my counsel be acceptable unto thee, and break off thy sins by righteousness, and thine iniquities by shewing mercy to the poor; if it may be a lengthening of thy tranquillity.*
>
> Daniel 4:24-27

The meaning of the dream was clear: if Nebuchadnezzar refused to recognize that his power had come from God and to give God glory for all the things that had been accomplished during the years of his reign, his kingdom would be taken from him. The following verse gives solemn notice of what happened next.

> *All this came upon the king Nebuchadnezzar.*
>
> Daniel 4:28

The judgment did not come immediately. God gave the king time to comply, to prove his love and loyalty to the King of Heaven. But twelve months later, the hammer fell — when it became apparent that Nebuchadnezzar would go the way of proud men:

> *At the end of twelve months he walked in the palace of the kingdom of Babylon. The king spake, and said, Is not this great Babylon, that I have built for the house of the kingdom by the might of MY power, and for the honour of MY majesty? While the word was in the king's mouth, there fell a voice from heaven, saying, O king Nebuchadnezzar, to thee it is spoken; The kingdom is departed from thee.* Daniel 4:29-31

Nebuchadnezzar was taking credit for all that God had done, and God cannot share His glory with man. The sentence was severe.

> *And they shall drive thee from men, and thy dwelling shall be with the beasts of the field: they shall make thee to eat grass as oxen, and seven times shall pass over thee, until thou know that the most High ruleth in the kingdom of men, and giveth it to whomsoever he will.*
>
> Daniel 4:32

And this time the result came immediately.

> *The same hour was the thing fulfilled upon*
> *Nebuchadnezzar: and he was driven from men,*
> *and did eat grass as oxen, and his body was wet*
> *with the dew of heaven, till his hairs were grown*
> *like eagles' feathers, and his nails like birds'*
> *claws.* Daniel 4:33

What a pitiful picture: a mighty king reduced to a mindless beast!

But Nebuchadnezzar did not lose all reason, and, in time, he came to himself and realized his error. Living with the wild beasts of the field, he had plenty of time to contemplate his mistake and to decide on a new course. In time, God restored his mind and his throne to him.

What a humbling experience! The words of the king reflect his new found humility.

> *And at the end of the days I Nebuchadnezzar*
> *lifted up mine eyes unto heaven, and mine un-*
> *derstanding returned unto me, and I blessed the*
> *most High, and I praised and honoured him that*
> *liveth for ever, whose dominion is an everlasting*
> *dominion, and his kingdom is from generation*
> *to generation: And all the inhabitants of the*
> *earth are reputed as nothing: and he doeth ac-*
> *cording to his will in the army of heaven, and*
> *among the inhabitants of the earth: and none can*
> *stay his hand, or say unto him, What doest*
> *thou? At the same time my reason returned*
> *unto me; and for the glory of my kingdom, mine*

*honour and brightness returned unto me; and
my counsellers and my lords sought unto me;
and I was established in my kingdom, and excel-
lent majesty was added unto me. Now I
Nebuchadnezzar praise and extol and honour
the King of heaven, all whose works are truth,
and his ways judgment: and those that walk in
pride he is able to abase.*   Daniel 4:34-37

How had Belshazzar responded to the knowledge
of what had happened to his father? He had done no
better than his father. In fact, he had committed a
sacrilege in taking the vessels dedicated to the use of
the Temple and used them to serve liquors to his
princes, his wives and his concubines. Not only had
they drunk from the sacred vessels; but, in their in-
ebriated state, they worshiped gods of gold and
silver.

*They drank wine, and praised the gods of gold,
and of silver, of brass, of iron, of wood, and of
stone.*   Daniel 5:4

It was then that the strange handwriting had come
on the wall.

*In the same hour came forth fingers of a man's
hand, and wrote over against the candlestick
upon the plaister of the wall of the king's palace:
and the king saw the part of the hand that wrote.*
Daniel 5:5

The story of Nebuchadnezzar's fall was no secret in Babylon. Daniel wasn't telling Belshazzar anything new. He had heard it all his life. Yet he had never applied it to his own life. Why is it that we always think our case is different? Daniel's words to Belshazzar were forceful:

> *And thou his son, O Belshazzar, hast not humbled thine heart, though thou knewest all this;*   Daniel 5:22

Why did Belshazzar succumb to pride? Why did he ignore the history of the past? Why did he rebel against the God of heaven and choose to defile sacred vessels and to worship pagan gods? Why indeed?

The handwriting was interpreted:

> *And this is the writing that was written, Mene, Mene, Tekel, Upharsin. This is the interpretation of the thing: Mene; God hath numbered thy kingdom, and finished it. Tekel; Thou art weighed in the balances, and art found wanting. Peres; Thy kingdom is divided, and given to the Medes and Persians. Then commanded Belshazzar, and they clothed Daniel with scarlet, and put a chain of gold about his neck, and made a proclamation concerning him, that he should be the third ruler in the kingdom.*
>   Daniel 5:25-29

That very night Belshazzar was slain by the Chaldeans.

> *In that night was Belshazzar the king of the Chaldeans slain.*   Daniel 5:30

What a powerful message! We must learn from the sad experiences of men and women like these. Heed the warning. God does not change. His word is consistent. What blessed one person will bless another; and what brought pain and tragedy to one person will surely do the same for another.

Let us each determine to stay humble before Almighty God and to give Him all glory and honor. For He alone is worthy.

It is the humble man or woman that God is seeking to *"stand in the gap,"* to *"make up the hedge,"* the man or woman willing to rely fully on the Lord, willing to empty himself of himself and fill himself with God's wisdom and understanding. Will you be that man or woman?

Let it not be said of you, *"I found none,"* rather let it be said of you, *"There is a man."* Learn to stay humble before God.   📖

📖

- 8 -

LEARN WHAT PLEASES GOD

Samuel also said unto Saul, The Lord sent me to anoint thee to be king over his people, over Israel: now therefore hearken thou unto the voice of the words of the Lord. Thus saith the Lord of hosts, I remember that which Amalek did to Israel, how he laid wait for him in the way, when he came up from Egypt. Now go and smite Amalek, and utterly destroy all that they have, and spare them not; but slay both man and woman, infant and suckling, ox and sheep, camel and ass.

1 Samuel 15:1-3

Saul was God's choice to be the first king of Israel, and the prophet Samuel was sent to anoint him for

the office. Samuel took with him specific instructions: Saul's first mission was to destroy God's
enemies, the Amalekites.

Saul prepared an army and went forth eagerly
against the Amalekites, and God gave him a great
victory. But Saul was not wholly faithful to his end of
the bargain.

> *But Saul and the people spared Agag, and the*
> *best of the sheep, and of the oxen, and of the*
> *fatlings, and the lambs, and all that was good,*
> *and would not utterly destroy them: but every*
> *thing that was vile and refuse, that they de-*
> *stroyed utterly.*   1 Samuel 15:9

God was not pleased with Saul's performance that
day. Yes, he had won the battle, but he had not honored God by recognizing that his victory was a result
of the Creator's power in his life. He had defied
God's express word in sparing Agag and some of the
animals for himself.

> *Then came the word of the Lord unto Samuel,*
> *saying, It repenteth me that I have set up Saul to*
> *be king: for he is turned back from following me,*
> *and hath not performed my commandments.*
> *And it grieved Samuel; and he cried unto the*
> *Lord all night.*   1 Samuel 15:10-11

It is sad when any man grieves the heart of God. It
is even more so when that man is a leader of the

people. The news saddened Samuel, and he *"cried unto the Lord all night."*

Some might be surprised at that reaction. They would picture Samuel as an angry prophet who delighted in pronouncing judgment on others. But that is a false concept of God's servants and of God Himself. Samuel did not wish Saul evil, and he did not pray for God to punish Saul. He wept for him, interceding for the king and seeking mercy from the Lord on his behalf.

We are so quick to judge others and feel that they should get "exactly what they deserve." The Spirit of Christ, however, is the Spirit of forgiveness, the Spirit of compassion, the Spirit which cries:

> *Father, forgive them; for they know not what they do.*   Luke 23:34

When we show mercy to others, God will show mercy to us. When we intercede for others, someone will be there to intercede for us — when we need it.

As with most people who err, Saul could not or would not recognize his wrong.

> *And Samuel came to Saul: and Saul said unto him, Blessed be thou of the Lord: I have performed the commandment of the Lord.*
> 1 Samuel 15:13

Samuel was not so sure.

And Samuel said, What meaneth then this bleat-
ing of the sheep in mine ears, and the lowing of
the oxen which I hear?   1 Samuel 15:14

As always, Saul had a ready answer:

They have brought them from the Amalekites:
for the people spared the best of the sheep and of
the oxen, to sacrifice unto the Lord thy God; and
the rest we have utterly destroyed.
                                    1 Samuel 15:15

Samuel felt compelled to point out the king's sin.

Then Samuel said unto Saul, Stay, and I will tell
thee what the Lord hath said to me this night.
And he said unto him, Say on. And Samuel said,
When thou wast little in thine own sight, wast
thou not made the head of the tribes of Israel, and
the Lord anointed thee king over Israel? And the
Lord sent thee on a journey, and said, Go and
utterly destroy the sinners the Amalekites, and
fight against them until they be consumed.
Wherefore then didst thou not obey the voice of
the Lord, but didst fly upon the spoil, and didst
evil in the sight of the Lord?
                                    1 Samuel 15:16-19

Saul answered a second time:

Yea, I have obeyed the voice of the Lord, and
have gone the way which the Lord sent me, and

have brought Agag the king of Amalek, and have
utterly destroyed the Amalekites.

1 Samuel 15:20

I have performed the commandment of the Lord.
I have obeyed the voice of the Lord.
I have gone the way which the Lord sent me.
I have utterly destroyed the Amalekites.

Saul wasn't man enough to admit that he had
sinned. When Samuel asked why he had spared
these animals, he replied, "the people spared the best
of the sheep and of the oxen, to sacrifice unto the
Lord thy God." He repeated his excuse.

But the people took of the spoil, sheep and oxen,
the chief of the things which should have been
utterly destroyed, to sacrifice unto the Lord thy
God in Gilgal. 1 Samuel 15:21

It is so much easier to shift the blame onto others
than to admit that we are guilty ourselves. I consider
Samuel's answer to King Saul to all this to be among
the most important passages of the entire Old Testament.

And Samuel said, Hath the Lord as great delight
in burnt offerings and sacrifices, as in obeying
the voice of the Lord? Behold, to obey is better
than sacrifice, and to hearken than the fat of
rams. For rebellion is as the sin of witchcraft,

and stubbornness is as iniquity and idolatry. Be-
cause thou hast rejected the word of the Lord, he
hath also rejected thee from being king.
                                        1 Samuel 15:22-23

We need to learn what causes God "delight," what
pleases Him. We are not to be guided by a set of rules
and regulations, but by the guiding principle of doing that which pleases the Lord.

At last, Saul admitted his guilt.

And Saul said unto Samuel, I have sinned: for I
have transgressed the commandment of the
Lord, and thy words: because I feared the people,
and obeyed their voice.   1 Samuel 15:24

Whether his "fear" of the people was legitimate or
whether it was just a pretext for his own failing, we
are not capable of saying. One thing is sure: fear is a
terrible thing. It is a destructive force. Fear even de-
stroys faith and can cause us to act in an irrational
manner.

We must also recognize, in the mix of evils that
destroyed Saul and ultimately caused him to lose the
kingdom, the insidious sin of pride. Pride is another
terribly destructive force. It separates us from God,
for it makes us think that we no longer need Him,
and thus damages our relationship with our Source
of all power. Pride will take over your decision making, as it did with Saul, and cause you to do what is
not convenient. He thought he could do God's will in
his own way, but he was wrong.

Saul was also a crowd pleaser. He didn't want to offend the people, but he didn't mind offending God. In the end, he thought that perhaps using the best of the animals as a sacrifice to God would appease Him, and, in this way, he could please everyone. But God let him know differently. God is looking for people who will *call* Him Lord and who will let Him *be* Lord in all their affairs.

Saul's failure caused him to be rejected and, soon, God brought David on the scene.

> *And the Lord said unto Samuel, How long wilt thou mourn for Saul, seeing I have rejected him from reigning over Israel? fill thine horn with oil, and go, I will send thee to Jesse the Bethlehemite: for I have provided me a king among his sons.* 1 Samuel 16:1

From the time of his youth, David had looked to the Lord to give him strength against every enemy. At first, it was a lion and, on another occasion, a bear. Later, it was to be the giant Goliath and the Philistines. God was pleased with David and sent Samuel to anoint him as king in Saul's stead.

Samuel supposed that the eldest son of Jesse would be the logical choice, but God chose the youngest son instead.

> *But the Lord said unto Samuel, Look not on his countenance, or on the height of his stature; because I have refused him: for the Lord seeth not*

> *as man seeth; for man looketh on the outward
> appearance, but the Lord looketh on the heart.*
>   1 Samuel 16:7

God knew who would stand against Goliath.
Where was "Eliab" when the Philistine raged? He
was trembling in fear with all the other "great men"
of Israel. No, the new king would not be taken from
among the battle-hardened warriors of the nation.
His chest was not draped with medals. He was taken
from the *sheepcote*, and he was perhaps an unlikely
choice, but he was God's choice, nevertheless.

Perhaps David was chosen because he did not
boast of what he could do, but boasted of the Lord's
goodness in his life. When Saul asked him why he
thought he could defeat the giant, he replied:

> *The Lord that delivered me out of the paw of the
> lion, and out of the paw of the bear, he will de-
> liver me out of the hand of this Philistine.*
>   1 Samuel 17:37

His brothers were not impressed. They accused
him of grandstanding and told him to go home to his
sheep.

> *And Eliab his eldest brother heard when he
> spake unto the men; and Eliab's anger was
> kindled against David, and he said, Why camest
> thou down hither? and with whom hast thou left
> those few sheep in the wilderness? I know thy*

pride, and the naughtiness of thine heart; for thou art come down that thou mightest see the battle. 1 Samuel 17:28

David's reply was very revealing.

Is there not a cause? 1 Samuel 17:29

He could not stand idly by and listen to this uncircumcised Philistine blaspheme the name of the Living God. Someone had to deal with the situation, and if no one else would do it, he would. In essence, he was offering himself up for the nation.

Just as he had put himself in the way of the bear and the lion, to protect the sheep entrusted to his care, he was now willing to put himself in harm's way for the sake of the people. That servant attitude gets God's attention every time. That's exactly the kind of man He is looking for.

There is so much wrong in our world today. Whole generations of young people are growing up without the benefit of having Bible reading and prayer in our public schools. And this has affected the moral fiber of our society. There is so much being taught to our young people that is opposed to godliness, so that many of our children are confused about the direction of their lives.

Families have always been the strength of the nation. But nowadays many parents are absent from home, and their children are required to make choices, with little or no parental guidance. They very often make wrong decisions. How could it be otherwise? But many parents are more concerned with moving up to a higher social position than with strengthening family relationships. We urgently need more Davids, men who will not follow the crowd, but will follow the Lord — no matter what the costs may be.

When word reached Saul of a young man who believed that the people of God could prevail against the Philistines, he immediately called for David, and when David stood before the king, his tongue did not fail him.

> *And David said to Saul, Let no man's heart fail because of him; thy servant will go and fight with this Philistine.*   1 Samuel 17:32

Just as fear is contagious, boldness (or lack of fear) is also contagious. Saul liked what he was hearing. The thing that puzzled him was that David was so young.

> *And Saul said to David, Thou art not able to go against this Philistine to fight with him: for thou art but a youth, and he a man of war from his youth.*   1 Samuel 17:33

It was then that David remembered the bear and the lion. Goliath, he was sure, would be no different.

> *Thy servant slew both the lion and the bear: and
> this uncircumcised Philistine shall be as one of
> them, seeing he hath defied the armies of the liv-
> ing God. The Lord that delivered me out of the
> paw of the lion, and out of the paw of the bear, he
> will deliver me out of the hand of this Philistine.*
> 1 Samuel 17:36-37

"He will deliver me." What more can be said?

David would have been foolish to make such boasts in himself. Young, small, unknown, inexperienced in warfare: he didn't have much going for him — in this world's way of thinking. He only had the Lord, but that proved to be more than enough. When he went out boldly to face the giant, God was with him and gave him a great deliverance. Goliath never had a chance. He had *"a sword," "a spear,"* and a *"shield"*; but David had the power of *"the name of the Lord of Hosts, the God of the armies of Israel."*

> *Then said David to the Philistine, Thou comest
> to me with a sword, and with a spear, and with a
> shield: but I come to thee in the name of the Lord
> of hosts, the God of the armies of Israel, whom
> thou hast defied.* 1 Samuel 17:45

Poor Goliath! He never had a chance.

God's people have nothing to fear. You, personally, have nothing to fear. You can be victorious in life. You can be at peace. You can be joyful. You can be confident. Just let God fight your battles for you.

David's greatest natural enemy in life turned out not to be Goliath, but King Saul, himself. When David was used of God to defeat the giant, he became so popular with the people that Saul became insanely jealous of him and never got over it. What is not apparent on the surface is that Saul was jealous of David because the young man had more of God's power than he did. It was easy to see that David was winning the hearts of the people and that he was destined to rule as king. That was not easy for Saul to swallow.

Although he had rewarded David by giving him his own daughter in marriage, Saul would now turn on David and would pursue him relentlessly for years, and God now had to protect David, not from bears or from Philistine giants, but from his own father-in-law.

With all this, David's heart was not embittered. Over a period of time, he had several opportunities to kill Saul, but he refused. He would not, he said, *"touch the Lord's anointed."*

> *And he said unto his men, The Lord forbid that I should do this thing unto my master, the Lord's anointed, to stretch forth mine hand against him, seeing he is the anointed of the Lord.*
>
> 1 Samuel 24:6

> *And David said to Abishai, Destroy him not: for who can stretch forth his hand against the Lord's anointed, and be guiltless?*
>
> 1 Samuel 26:9

The Lord forbid that I should stretch forth mine hand against the Lord's anointed: but, I pray thee, take thou now the spear that is at his bolster, and the cruse of water, and let us go.
                                          1 Samuel 26:11

In the end, Saul destroyed himself and his sons. By consulting with the witch of Endor, thus making the devil his source of information and not the Lord, he removed himself from the Lord's protection, and was soon killed.

David became the King of Judah, and although not everyone honored him at first, God kept him strong against his enemies.

But our greatest enemies are not always Philistines, and the greatest danger to our soul sometimes comes when we stay home from the battle. David was about to face his greatest moment of trial.

And it came to pass, after the year was expired, at the time when kings go forth to battle, that David sent Joab, and his servants with him, and all Israel; and they destroyed the children of Ammon, and besieged Rabbah. But David tarried still at Jerusalem. And it came to pass in an eveningtide, that David arose from off his bed, and walked upon the roof of the king's house: and from the roof he saw a woman washing herself; and the woman was very beautiful to look upon. And David sent and inquired after the woman. And one said, Is not this Bathsheba, the

*daughter of Eliam, the wife of Uriah the Hittite?
And David sent messengers, and took her; and
she came in unto him, and he lay with her; for
she was purified from her uncleanness: and she
returned unto her house. And the woman conceived, and sent and told David, and said, I am
with child.   2 Samuel 11:1-5*

David's strength had always been revealed in
battle, and he had no business staying home now.
Avoiding a fight and taking the easy way out led him
right into temptation and grief. It doesn't pay to be in
the wrong place at the wrong time.

For a king who had so many subjects at his beck
and call, it would have seemed easy for David to
cover his sin, but God would not allow it. Perhaps
some of David's subjects were deceived, but in the
end God sent a prophet, Nathan, to show David that
He, at least, was not. Nathan told David a quaint
story.

*And the Lord sent Nathan unto David. And he
came unto him, and said unto him, There were
two men in one city; the one rich, and the other
poor. The rich man had exceeding many flocks
and herds: But the poor man had nothing, save
one little ewe lamb, which he had bought and
nourished up: and it grew up together with him,
and with his children; it did eat of his own meat,
and drank of his own cup, and lay in his bosom,
and was unto him as a daughter. And there came*

*a traveller unto the rich man, and he spared to
take of his own flock and of his own herd, to
dress for the wayfaring man that was come unto
him; but took the poor man's lamb, and dressed
it for the man that was come to him.*
2 Samuel 12:1-4

David was furious and demanded to know what
man had dared to exhibit such callous behavior. He
would surely punish the man, and justly so.
Nathan's answer was chilling and unforgettable.

Thou art the man. 2 Samuel 12:7

The reaction of David in this very tense moment is
all important. Other powerful men, in David's position, had prophets imprisoned and killed for lesser
accusations. What would David do? Rather than re-
act angrily and violently against the prophet, he
realized how true the prophet's words were and decided that he had had enough of sin. He repented,
and was rewarded.

*And David said unto Nathan, I have sinned
against the Lord. And Nathan said unto David,
The Lord also hath put away thy sin; thou shalt
not die.* 2 Samuel 12:13

I have sinned. That's all God needed to hear. That is
all He requires. David was forgiven. He would pay
dearly for his sin, but, because he had repented and

sought God's forgiveness, his sin would not hinder
his relationship to God. From that day on, David realized just how very weak he was without the Lord
and continually cried out for God's strength, so that
he might remain pure.

> *Create in me a clean heart, O God; and renew a*
> *right spirit within me. Cast me not away from*
> *thy presence; and take not thy Holy Spirit from*
> *me. Restore unto me the joy of thy salvation; and*
> *uphold me with thy free spirit.*
>
> Psalms 51:10-12

God heard and answered that prayer, and David
made up his mind that with the Lord's help he
would never again stray.

We can all take heart from David's story and know
that no matter how far we may have strayed from the
loving arms of the Savior, He is always reaching out
to us. As the father waited in the field, anxious for the
return of his prodigal son, and ready to receive him
again, our heavenly Father extends to each of us a
welcome to live eternally with him. Let us each have
a made-up mind, as David did, to never more stray
from the presence of the Father. And may each of us
be concerned, from day to day, with living a life
pleasing to Him.   📖

- 9 -

LEARN TO APPRECIATE THE LOVE OF GOD

What is man, that thou art MINDFUL of him?
and the son of man, that thou visitest him?
Psalms 8:4

What a wonderful truth was brought forth by the Psalmist! The God of all creation and Master of the Universe is mindful of us. We are in His thoughts and under His constant care. He has our best interests at heart and is looking out for our welfare. That is good news!

When Jesus came into the world, it was because He was mindful of our need of redemption from sin. He was keenly aware of our lost condition and knew that we could not help ourselves. He was willing to give up, for a time, the glories of heaven (which surpass anything we have ever seen or known in this world), for us. From the foundations of the world, Father God had a plan, so remarkable that no man could ever deny that only He could have conceived of it: to send His Son to earth, to die for the sins of men.

Jesus was sent to *"visit"* man. And, amazingly, He came as a man, lived here as a man, suffered as a man, and, as a man, took the curse of our sins upon Himself. Oh, wondrous story!

Jesus knew rejection:

> *He came unto his own, and his own received him*
> *not.*   John 1:11

What a sad commentary!

He came to this world with a mandate to first redeem His own, but His own people rejected His offer — because He didn't fit their pattern of what a Messiah should be. He wasn't born to royalty and didn't even have a white horse.

But, in His rejection, Jesus extended His arms of love to all mankind:

> *But as many as received him, to them gave he*
> *power to become the sons of God, even to them*
> *that believe on his name:*   John 1:12

Still, He is mindful of His people, the Jews, and has never turned His back on them. Paul would later declare:

> *God hath not cast away his people which he fore-*
> *knew. Wot ye not what the scripture saith of*

Elias? how he maketh intercession to God against Israel, saying,   Romans 11:2

I say then, Have they stumbled that they should fall? God forbid: but rather through their fall salvation is come unto the Gentiles, for to provoke them to jealousy.   Romans 11:11

Now if the fall of them be the riches of the world, and the diminishing of them the riches of the Gentiles; how much more their fulness? For I speak to you Gentiles, inasmuch as I am the apostle of the Gentiles, I magnify mine office: If by any means I may provoke to emulation them which are my flesh, and might save some of them. For if the casting away of them be the reconciling of the world, what shall the receiving of them be, but life from the dead?   Romans 11:12-15

For if the firstfruit be holy, the lump is also holy: and if the root be holy, so are the branches. And if some of the branches be broken off, and thou, being a wild olive tree, wert graffed in among them, and with them partakest of the root and fatness of the olive tree; Boast not against the branches. But if thou boast, thou bearest not the root, but the root thee. Thou wilt say then, The branches were broken off, that I might be graffed in. Well; because of unbelief they were broken off, and thou standest by faith. Be not high-

> *minded, but fear: For if God spared not the natu-*
> *ral branches, take heed lest he also spare not*
> *thee.* Romans 11:16-21

Blessings are promised to those who follow the Lord carefully and warnings are expressed to those who would be high minded. Let every one of us be aware of the fact that anyone can be cut off. Israel has suffered *"blindness in part."*

> *For I would not, brethren, that ye should be ig-*
> *norant of this mystery, lest ye should be wise in*
> *your own conceits; that blindness in part is hap-*
> *pened to Israel, until the fulness of the Gentiles*
> *be come in.* Romans 11:25

Yes, God is mindful of His people and sent Jesus to die on Calvary's cross, to become the ultimate sacrifice for you and me. Any "sacrifice" we may have made to serve Him pales in comparison. In the early part of my Christian experience, I considered that I had made great sacrifices to serve the Lord, but the longer I serve Him, the more I am aware of His continual care for me. Now, I realize that I gave up nothing to gain everything. Following Jesus is not a sacrifice. It is the greatest privilege that any man could be given.

John expressed it well:

> *Behold, what manner of love the Father hath be-*
> *stowed upon us, that we should be called the*

*sons of God: therefore the world knoweth us not,
because it knew him not. Beloved, now are we
the sons of God, and it doth not yet appear what
we shall be: but we know that, when he shall
appear, we shall be like him; for we shall see him
as he is.*   1 John 3:1-2

Because of His great love, because He is ever mindful of us, we can face any attack of the enemy of our
souls. We can remain strong in the face of temptation
or Satan's attempts to afflict us with sickness or discouragement. Because of God's care for us, we will
not be overcome; we will be overcomers.

Because of the mindfulness of God, we need not
worry as other people do. We need not look at life in
the same terms as those who are without hope and
without God's loving care. His mindfulness frees us
of needless concern for the things of this world. For
instance, it is said of the great heroes of faith recorded in Hebrews 11 that they were not *"mindful"* of
their former state.

*And truly, if they had been mindful of that
country from whence they came out, they might
have had opportunity to have returned.*
                                           Hebrews 11:15

These men and women went through great
testings and trials and yet did not turn away from the
course that the Lord had set for them. Their minds
had taken a new course. Being "mindful," in this

sense, means looking back, considering their life before they had decided to "endure all things" for the prize of eternal life. So many people continually live in the past, continually long to return to a former existence — especially when things get difficult.

These men and women were asked to do hard things (impossible things, to man's way of thinking), yet they did not hesitate.

Abraham and Sarah were among those who were not mindful of the former life.

> *By faith Abraham, when he was called to go out into a place which he should after receive for an inheritance, obeyed; and he went out, not knowing whither he went. By faith he sojourned in the land of promise, as in a strange country, dwelling in tabernacles with Isaac and Jacob, the heirs with him of the same promise: For he looked for a city which hath foundations, whose builder and maker is God. Through faith also Sara herself received strength to conceive seed, and was delivered of a child when she was past age, because she judged him faithful who had promised. Therefore sprang there even of one, and him as good as dead, so many as the stars of the sky in multitude, and as the sand which is by the sea shore innumerable.*   Hebrews 11:8-12

Abraham was called out of the familiar and into the unfamiliar, and "he went out." He didn't know where he was going, but he trusted the goodness of the God who had called him. Consequently, he *"received the inheritance."*

> *He staggered not at the promise of God through*
> *unbelief; but was strong in faith, giving glory to*
> *God;*   Romans 4:20

The crowning verse of the faith chapter is verse 13:

> *These all died in faith, not having received the*
> *promises, but having seen them afar off, and*
> *were persuaded of them, and embraced them,*
> *and confessed that they were strangers and pil-*
> *grims on the earth.*   Hebrews 11:13

"These all died in faith." They faced every test and never looked back. With single-minded determination, they endured until the end. They were not "mindful" of what might have been or what they might have lost by serving the Lord. His mindfulness freed them of these concerns so common to man.

Each of us will be tempted to go back to where we came from. When troubles come to us, our enemy will remind us of the "good old days" and try to entice us to go back to the world. If our minds are full of worldly thoughts and worldly ambitions, he just might succeed. But if our minds are fixed on the goodness of God, we will surely follow the Lord and not look back.

Chapter 12 of Hebrews opens with these words:

Wherefore seeing we also are compassed about with so great a cloud of witnesses, let us lay aside every weight, and the sin which doth so easily beset us, and let us run with patience the race that is set before us,   Hebrews 12:1

This *"great cloud of witnesses"* in chapter 12 is made up of the saints written about in chapter 11. They want to tell us all: "You can make it. God is on your side. We endured and so can you. Nothing can stop you. Hold on to the end and you will have an eternal reward waiting for you."

The Lord is mindful of us. Let us not desire the former life but press on to receive the fulness of His glory.   📖

- 10 -

LEARN THE POWER OF WORDS

A Soft answer turneth away wrath: but grievous words stir up anger.   Proverbs 15:1

Words are powerful. They not only give expression to our thoughts, they often take on a life of their own. Words can strengthen, as in the case of strengthening relationships, relationships with loved ones or family members, with friends, with colleagues, with government representatives and with business associates. And words can destroy.

Jesus said:

But I say unto you, That every idle word that men shall speak, they shall give account thereof in the day of judgment. For by thy words thou shalt be justified, and by thy words thou shalt be condemned.   Matthew 12:36-37

Words are important because if the meaning of what we want to communicate is expressed correctly it will usually be received in a favorable way by those who hear it. If there is some fault in the way the words are communicated, however, our communications can result in misunderstandings, hurt feelings, and a drawing back on the part of the people addressed.

The wrong words or the right words spoken in the wrong way can mean lost friendships, broken hearts, lost business opportunities and, in the case of governments, the breaking off of diplomatic relations. In the extreme case, wrong words can even cause wars.

Obviously, then, developing communicating skills is important to each of us to enable us to maintain better relations with the people around us. As Christians, communication is even more important because we want to communicate the gospel message in a way pleasing to the Lord.

The book of Proverbs, a book of God's wisdom, has much to say about the matter of communication. It was King Solomon who taught us the importance of *"a soft answer."* He was absolutely right. Nothing engenders peace more quickly. There is much to be gained by responding with *a soft answer.*

Grievous, painful or hurtful words will surely stir up anger in the other party and will damage relationships. Think before you speak. Ask God to give you

His grace so that you can be more gentle in your speech.

> *Pleasant words are as an honeycomb, sweet to the soul, and health to the bones.*
> Proverbs 16:24

This verse says it even better. *"Pleasant words"* not only work to strengthen relationships, but they are beneficial to the person speaking them. They bring *"health to the bones."*

In the same way, grievous words not only damage relationships, they are harmful to the health of the person who speaks them. Therefore, let us all strive to use *"pleasant"* and *"soft"* speech for the benefit of our relationships and for our own good health and well being.

> *Death and life are in the power of the tongue: and they that love it shall eat the fruit thereof.*
> Proverbs 18:21

This is one of the most important verses in a very important book. If we could fully grasp the significance of this short passage, we would surely be more careful in what we say to one another. Isn't it amazing to think that the words we speak can bring either life or death to a situation! The difference between success or failure, therefore, may just be our choice of words.

An interesting test might be to record the dinner table conversation in your home one evening and then play it back. You might be quite amazed by the number of negative comments that are made during the course of a simple meal. Negativism in our speech is one of the most important elements that prevents us from being as effective as we could be in the service of the Lord.

God said to the people of Moses' day:

> *See, I have set before thee this day life and good,*
> *and death and evil;*   Deuteronomy 30:15

This subject of death and life in the power of the tongue is particularly important in our relationship with our mate and our children. If men continually compare their wives to their mothers — in regard to her cooking or keeping house, her appearance or intelligence, or, worse yet, her spending habits — they could "have a tiger by the tail." Such unwise use of words often causes an otherwise healthy marriage to go into a tailspin. And it happens every day.

"You're just like your mother!"

The tone of voice used to make this type of comment makes it very obvious that it wasn't meant to be a compliment, and there is no faster way to kill a marriage than to make such statements. The same can be true if a wife makes hurtful comparisons between her husband and her father. It is always destructive to make critical comments about weaknesses, perceived or real, in your spouse's family.

A lack of social grace in this regard, a lack of education on the matter, or improper use of language to communicate ideas or feelings, can all lead to disaster.

Children often grow up with attitudes of inferiority because of words spoken over them by their parents as they were growing up.

> *You're so dumb!*
> *You'll never amount to anything!*
> *Why can't you be like your brother?*
> *How can your sister be so musically talented, and when you play it sounds like a cat is running over the piano keys?*

This type of comparison is not helpful, and making such statements is one of the most destructive forces in husband-wife relationships and parent-child relationships. Each one of us is an individual, a very different individual, with individual talents and abilities. Why compare one to the other? Each individual must be treated as a unique person. We are each the product of the words that were spoken over us during our formative years, and words continue to affect us.

In marriage, words are everything, and when children are involved, those words affect them too — very deeply. When a husband or wife criticizes or demeans their partner in front of their children, this causes confusion in the minds of the children. These encounters cause insecurities and frustrations. Children don't know how to handle these conflicts. Every child wants to love both his mother and his father, but when there is open bickering in his presence, he is forced to take sides. Changing his attitude of respect for one of his parents then often causes deep feelings of guilt within the child. He even begins to think that something he did has caused this rupture of relationships.

If even discussing some of these hurtful phrases that are commonly used makes us uncomfortable, how much more pain they cause us when we actually experience their destructive force.

As Proverbs is the book of wisdom of the Old Testament, so James is the book of wisdom of the New Testament; and James also has some very strong comments about the tongue.

> *And the tongue is a fire, a world of iniquity: so is the tongue among our members, that it defileth the whole body, and setteth on fire the course of nature; and it is set on fire of hell. For every kind of beasts, and of birds, and of serpents, and of things in the sea, is tamed, and hath been tamed of mankind: But the tongue can no man tame; it is an unruly evil, full of deadly poison. Therewith bless we God, even the Father; and therewith curse we men, which are made after the similitude of God. Out of the same mouth proceedeth blessing and cursing. My brethren, these things ought not so to be.*   James 3:6-10

Either blessing or cursing can come forth from the same mouth. In this way, your mouth is a creative force or a destructive force. Learn to guard your tongue against saying abusive words and speaking forth things that will inflict wounds on others. This is not just a matter of holding your hand over your mouth, for what is in our hearts is manifested in our speech. But as we spend more time in the Word of God, in reading and meditating on His thoughts, our speech will become more gentle and pleasing to Him. And we will become the kind of person who draws others into a relationship with Jesus Christ — by their words.

> *A word fitly spoken is like apples of gold in pictures of silver.* Proverbs 25:11

> *My son, attend to my words; incline thine ear unto my sayings. Let them not depart from thine eyes; keep them in the midst of thine heart. For they are life unto those that find them, and health to all their flesh.* Proverbs 4:20-22

Godly words bring life and health, while hurtful, critical and judgmental words bring pain, discouragement, anger and unforgiveness. If a person is continually harangued with such negative words, it eventually affects their feelings of self-worth, security and trust. People who suffer so even begin to question whether life is worth living.

> *Thou art snared with the words of thy mouth,*
> *thou art taken with the words of thy mouth.*
>   Proverbs 6:2

If we say we can't, then we can't. If we say some-thing is impossible for us, then it will be impossible for us. If we say we will probably get the flu this winter, we will surely get the flu. If we say we will probably be passed over for a promotion, it will hap-pen just as we have said. It is a rather scary thought, but the words we speak actually produce results in our life.

Why should we say, **I can't**, when the Bible says:

> *I can do all things through Christ which*
> *strengtheneth me.*   Philippians 4:13

It is not prideful to say, **I can**. We know that we can do nothing at all in ourselves. But when the Lord is on our side, nothing is impossible to us. I can do whatever the Lord has called me to do. And so can you.

> *All the words of my mouth are in righteousness;*
> *there is nothing froward or perverse in them.*
>   Proverbs 8:8

The Lord is our example in this regard. His words are righteous, and ours should be, too. His words are not *"froward or perverse,"* not mean or hurtful. Ours should be like that, as well.

The mouth of a righteous man is a well of life:
but violence covereth the mouth of the wicked.
Proverbs 10:11

In rural areas of the world, where much of the world's population lives, there is nothing more vital than a good well. In this verse, *"the mouth of the righteous"* is compared to such a well. That is not surprising since wells provide life-giving and life-sustaining water. The mouth can be *"a well of life."* It is not only life-giving, but it is refreshing. The words of a righteous man should be a blessing and a strength to those around him.

The words of the wicked, as we all know, are perverse, devious and self-seeking. And those perverse words often lead him to perverse deeds. *"Violence covererth [his] mouth."*

Some of Solomon's wise teachings about the power of words need no commentary:

> *Lying lips are abomination to the Lord: but they*
> *that deal truly are his delight.* Proverbs 12:22

> *He that keepeth his mouth keepeth his life: but he*
> *that openeth wide his lips shall have destruction.*
> Proverbs 13:3

> *Pleasant words are as an honeycomb, sweet to*
> *the soul, and health to the bones.*
> Proverbs 16:24

The words of a talebearer are as wounds, and they go down into the innermost parts of the belly.   Proverbs 18:8

Seest thou a man that is hasty in his words? there is more hope of a fool than of him.
                    Proverbs 29:20

Words affect us and everyone around us.

When I was writing my thesis for my doctorate degree in Dental School, I chose the subject "The Psychosomatic Aspects of Dentistry." Simply stated, this means using simple means to make the dental procedure more pleasant for the patient. I had already realized that anything I could do to make the dental procedure more comfortable would benefit the patient and cause them to be a walking advertisement for my dental practice. The patient would benefit, and I would benefit. Because I would build a reputation as a painless dentist, I would have more patients and more frequent and consistent visits from my patients, and my pocket book would benefit, as a result.

As with all medical science, dentistry has made great advances in recent years. Many aids have been developed to alleviate pain. One of those that I used effectively is called "audio analgesia" or "white sound." It simply means providing the patient with earphones connected to a stereo tape system and allowing them to select the type of music they want to listen to and to control the volume of the music. When they begin to experience any discomfort, they can turn up a second volume control and a sound, such as a waterfall, will be introduced. Amazingly, this distracts the patient to the point that they focus more on the sound and less on the discomfort of the procedure. We found this to be more useful with some patients than with others. It was particularly effective with children.

Topical anesthetics, a substance rubbed on the gum to numb the area before injections, proved to be a great help for many patients. We began using disposable syringes so that the tip of the needle was always sharp. We would even sometimes sedate overly anxious patients to relax them for the dental visit, using Nitrous Oxide anesthesia (once called laughing gas).

We also found it helpful to remove from the treatment rooms anything that smelled or looked like a doctor's office or a hospital. This, too, helped patients relax.

Over and above all these medical techniques, the most important element in our rapport with our patients was the tone of our conversation with them and our choice of words. We were very careful NEVER to use words that would cause fear, particularly in children. Since a good percentage of our patients were children, we had to learn how to get them to trust us and not have any fear of coming for their regular dental visits.

Parents who brought their children in were not always helpful in this regard. A mother might say, "Go on in, Jimmy. He's not going to hurt you." And that simple statement would set off alarm bells in the child. Hurt? Who said anything about hurt? Invariably, the child started to cry. Hurt ... pain ... shots ... drills ... needle ... blood ... faint ... dizzy: these were all words that we NEVER used because they instilled fear in a patient and, afterward, we had a hard time getting them quieted down again. It was very important to keep mothers out of the treatment room because they could upset their children with the wrong choice of words.

We had great success with children when we could teach the mother how to prepare her child for a dental visit. The child had to look forward to the visit as something pleasant, and had to see us as his or her friends. If not, we all suffered.

I learned so many important lessons in those days about dealing with people and about choosing the right words. As a dentist, our words had the power to strengthen our relationship with a patient and to establish their confidence or to cause fear in the person — to the point that they would avoid visiting the dentist at all costs. This latter result, of course, was detrimental both to them and to us.

This is not meant to be a lesson in dentistry. What I am trying to point out is that when there is a profit motive involved we take very seriously our responsibility to make the people around us feel comfortable. But, just as words are important in a medical setting, so they are important in interpersonal relationships: marriages, friendship, business dealings, in church settings and in ministries.

It is not easy to always speak encouraging and helpful words. Our nature may be to do the opposite. We all need God's help in this regard, but He is ever ready to extend that help and to cause us to speak blessing and life to one another. The sooner you learn the power of words the better off you will be in every regard. 📖

- 11 -

LEARN THE IMPORTANCE OF WORK

So built we the wall; and all the wall was joined together unto the half thereof: for the people had a mind to work. Nehemiah 4:6

We have so much to learn from Nehemiah and his coworkers. These people had a purpose in life and didn't stop working at it until they had completed the project, despite every difficulty they faced.

Now, the Bible is very realistic, and it doesn't pretend that people are perfect. Among all the Bible characters, there are very few examples of men or women who did not fail God in some way. Joseph and Daniel were two examples of those who wholly followed the Lord. There is no evidence that either of them ever turned away from God. And Nehemiah falls into that category too.

This man Nehemiah had a very trusted position in the court of the Persian king Artaxerxes. He was the king's cupbearer. That might not sound like a very important position, but kings had many enemies and constantly had to be on guard to protect themselves from those who would do them harm. Putting poison in the king's cup was one of the most common threats of such enemies. So, to make a man his cupbearer, the king had to have confidence in that man. Thus, Nehemiah had access to the king.

One day, some of his fellow Jews, who were among the small remnant that returned to the land of Judah from captivity, came to visit him. When he asked them about the homeland and how the people were faring, the report they gave made him extremely sad.

> *The remnant that are left of the captivity there in the province are in great affliction and reproach: the wall of Jerusalem also is broken down, and the gates thereof are burned with fire.*
>   Nehemiah 1:3

It was bad enough to have spent years in captivity, but to return home, after many years of suffering thus, and to find the city in this condition must have been very depressing for these people. But Nehemiah had absolutely no logical reason to get involved in the problems of the people of faraway

Judah. Because of his trusted position, Nehemiah was doing well in life. He owed the people of Judah nothing. An offering of sympathy would probably have been considered sufficient, and Nehemiah could have gotten back to his work.

Nehemiah, however, had a very different reaction. He was deeply saddened by this news, almost as if he had suffered the calamities himself.

> *And it came to pass, when I heard these words, that I sat down and wept, and mourned certain days, and fasted, and prayed before the God of heaven,* Nehemiah 1:4

This was no passing mood. If anything, Nehemiah's sadness deepened with time, a sadness that convinced him that he must do something about this deplorable situation. He prayed about it *"day and night,"* allowing the severity of the situation to draw him closer to God and cause him to confess his own sins and the sins of his people. Repentance, he remembered, was a prerequisite to God's promise to redeem His people and cause them to return to the land. And he reminded God of that fact.

> *Remember, I beseech thee, the word that thou commandedst thy servant Moses, saying, If ye transgress, I will scatter you abroad among the nations: But if ye turn unto me, and keep my commandments, and do them; though there were of you cast out unto the uttermost part of the*

*heaven, yet will I gather them from thence, and
will bring them unto the place that I have chosen
to set my name there.*   Nehemiah 1:8-9

But what was Nehemiah's role to be in this thing
God was doing? He was convinced that his world
was about to be turned upside down and that he
needed God to move upon the heart of the king to
grant him permission to go and do whatever it was
God was calling him to do.

Soon afterward, the king noticed the sadness upon
the countenance of his cupbearer. He had probably
never even taken notice of his servant's moods before this. Now, for some strange reason, he was
interested and asked about it, opening a door to
Nehemiah to seek the permission he desired.

When Nehemiah told his master about the deplorable condition of his people, the king asked:

For what dost thou make request?
                                        Nehemiah 2:4

Had Nehemiah said anything about requesting
something? I don't think so. God was moving on the
heart of the king. He was not only interested in the
burden of his cupbearer, but he now wanted to do
something to help out. What a miracle! Prayer
changes things!

I like what Nehemiah did next.

So I prayed to the God of heaven.
                                        Nehemiah 2:4

Why was Nehemiah praying again, although he had spent many days and nights in prayer? It is a fearful thing to face a king who could just as easily have you beheaded as to grant you some unusual permission. Nehemiah was a slave. He had no rights. God had to help him in this moment.

He boldly asked the king for permission to go to Jerusalem and help rebuild the city walls. What did a cupbearer know about reconstructing a city? When God calls us, we can do what He has destined us to do, we can do it well, and we can do it quickly.

The king asked how long would it take him to rebuild the city and return. What did a cupbearer know about how long it would take to do any of this? Nothing! But he knew God, and that changes everything.

Amazingly, the permission Nehemiah sought was granted. The king trusted this man. That speaks well of Nehemiah and of his God.

Nehemiah took the opportunity and made two more requests. He needed letters from the governors of the territories through which he would pass on his way back to Jerusalem, so that they would give him safe conduct and not delay his journey or detain him. And he needed a letter to the keeper of the royal forests to give him timber for the rebuilding project. When both of these requests were immediately granted, Nehemiah knew it was God who had done it. He said:

And the king granted me, according to the good hand of my God upon me.   Nehemiah 2:8

How remarkable! There is no evidence to suggest that this king had a personal relationship with Nehemiah's God. Why, then, would he agree to this plan? There was no prolonged discussion about rights, no demands that Nehemiah serve the king instead of dashing off on some wild goose chase. "Granted!" the king said. What a miracle!

When we are faithful, God rewards that faithfulness. Nehemiah soon found himself on his way to the Holy City, accompanied by *"captains of the army"* sent by the king to convey his cupbearer in safety. Hallelujah!

Not everyone was happy about the prospect of the rebuilding of the walls of Jerusalem. When Sanballat and his servant Tobiah heard of Nehemiah's plan, they were grieved that anyone wanted to help the Israelites. When God has a plan, the devil always tries to block it. Nehemiah knew that opposition must come, and he pressed on to Jerusalem.

When Nehemiah arrived in the city, what he saw must have been devastating. For three days he did nothing. I can imagine that many wild thoughts had been running through his mind:

> *Was he insane thinking that he could rebuild this rubble? What did he know about building? He was a cupbearer. Where would he start? Could it even be done? Had he been wrong to give the king a time when he would be back? What had possessed him to think that he could*

*do so much in such a short time or get the people
involved in the project?*

But Nehemiah didn't turn around and go home, as
many would have done. He didn't say "impossible."
He didn't make excuses. He sought God and carefully began to form a plan. This project needed a lot
of prayer and a lot of thought. Don't jump in before
you know what you are doing.

He hadn't yet discussed the project with other men
(a mistake that we often make). He didn't want to
hear any discouraging comments or be swayed by
the thoughts of what was and wasn't possible. He
wanted to hear from God first.

On the third night, he got up during the night and
took a ride around the city to survey the damage. At
one point, the rubble was piled so high that there was
no place for him to pass with his *"beast."* What he
saw was not encouraging.

> *The walls ... were broken down*
> *The gates ... were consumed with fire.*
> Nehemiah 2:13

Words cannot convey the sense of what Nehemiah
saw and felt that night. *"Broken down"* and *"consumed"* are powerful phrases that conjure up vivid
images. But the sight of it, the reality of it was much
worse.

When Nehemiah was satisfied that he had a plan
from God, he then called together the people of the

city to tell them what God had laid upon his heart. Many people can see a problem, but few can see a solution.

> *Then said I unto them, Ye see the distress that we are in, how Jerusalem lieth waste, and the gates thereof are burned with fire: come, and let us build up the wall of Jerusalem, that we be no more a reproach. Then I told them of the hand of my God which was good upon me; as also the king's words that he had spoken unto me. And they said, Let us rise up and build. So they strengthened their hands for this good work.*
>
> Nehemiah 2:17-18

To underscore his message and to give it weight, Nehemiah told the people how God had moved upon the king and made his coming possible, about the accompanying guard, the letters of safe passage to the governors and the permission to use the royal timbers.

That was a wise way to begin, for Nehemiah must have surely known what was in the hearts of the people, what they were thinking:

> *This is an impossible situation. There is no way out of this dilemma. We simply do not have the ability to rebuild this wall. We don't have enough skilled laborers or finances for materials or experience in such projects. Forget it. This is too much to expect of us.*

When God sends you to help people, you first have to overcome their reluctance to believe that they can be helped. The method Nehemiah used worked. The people were inspired and said to Nehemiah, *"Let us rise up and build,"* and, as a result, *"they strengthened their hands for this good work."* If you can inspire other people to action, there is no limit to what you can accomplish for God.

These people had been discouraged and disheartened, but when a man of vision came into their midst, things began to change immediately. They caught the vision and were ready and anxious to get on with the project.

That didn't mean that everything was going to flow smoothly. Just when things began to get underway, Sanballat and Tobiah showed up to try to dampen the spirits of the people. They did it by laughing and mocking and showing their scorn for those who would attempt such a project with such limited resources. They even suggested that the Jews were planning a rebellion against the king. The devil will say the most absurd thing imaginable to try to intimidate us. But Nehemiah had an answer for these men.

> *Then answered I them, and said unto them, The God of heaven, he will prosper us; therefore we his servants will arise and build: but ye have no portion, nor right, nor memorial, in Jerusalem.*
> Nehemiah 2:20

That was the end of that discussion — for the moment. And the work was undertaken with a vengeance.

Each family was assigned a task, the rebuilding of a certain gate or a certain portion of the wall. The task was monumental, but if each family would concentrate on just one portion of the task and not interfere with what others were doing, it could be done.

The responsibility of Nehemiah to oversee the whole project was amazingly great. Consider that there were 42,360 workers, plus 7,337 servants and (most importantly) 245 singers. In such a group you would find every conceivable type of personality and temperament to be dealt with.

In a group that size, there must have been many who would have liked to think they knew better than Nehemiah how to do this thing and who, perhaps, wanted to rise up against his authority and take charge. In a group so large it is not difficult to imagine some of the squabbles and divisions that could have easily resulted and wrecked the whole project, leaving it half finished. The fact that it didn't happen is a tribute to God's wisdom, to Nehemiah's leadership, and to the people's willingness to work. They *"had a mind to work."*

When you know that what you are doing is the plan of God, and when you follow that plan with a determination to see the project through to the end, God will help you — no matter who is against you.

The devil had not given up. He was greatly distressed, seeing the walls of the Holy City rise again.

> *But it came to pass, that when Sanballat heard that we builded the wall, he was wroth, and took great indignation, and mocked the Jews. And he spake before his brethren and the army of Samaria, and said, What do these feeble Jews? will they fortify themselves? will they sacrifice? will they make an end in a day? will they revive the stones out of the heaps of the rubbish which are burned? Now Tobiah the Ammonite was by him, and he said, Even that which they build, if a fox go up, he shall even break down their stone wall.*   Nehemiah 4:1-3

But the people of God just kept right on building. They didn't have time to entertain these insults. They had a job to do.

Certainly every pastor, youth leader and mission director alive today would love to be able to say that he had people like Nehemiah's, those who have *"a mind to work,"* a mind to accomplish something important for the Kingdom of God. We need more single-minded and willing people. We have a mission given to us by the Lord to get the Gospel out to a lost and dying generation. On every hand, there are souls to be won, sick bodies to be healed, and demon possessed people to be freed. It is not enough, however, to have a great vision and a great desire to do the work. We must believe God to help us motivate the people around us to help reap the harvest. We have to get out in the field and work.

As the work progressed, the enemies of God and His people began to make physical attacks upon the workers. Guards had to be set night and day to warn of their approach. In some locations along the wall, half of the workers were assigned to fight while the other half took arms to defend the whole group against the enemy attacks. In still other locations the workers kept their tools in one hand and their weapons in the other and kept right on working.

When Nehemiah saw that some small family groups were isolated in the area in which they were working and might become easy targets for the enemy, he devised a plan for their protection. Everyone was to continue to work in small family groups, but if they found themselves threatened by outsiders, they were to blow a trumpet, advising the other families nearby that they needed help.

> *And I said unto the nobles, and to the rulers, and to the rest of the people, The work is great and large, and we are separated upon the wall, one far from another. In what place therefore ye hear the sound of the trumpet, resort ye thither unto us: our God shall fight for us.*
>
> Nehemiah 4:19-20

When anyone heard the trumpet call for help, they were to rush to the assistance of the other family. What a wonderful plan of defense!

Because of the urgency of the task, the people were expected to work long hours.

> *So we laboured in the work ... from the rising of the morning till the stars appeared.*
> Nehemiah 4:21

In fact, they were so dedicated to what they were doing that they rarely took time to change clothes, except to wash them.

> *So neither I, nor my brethren, nor my servants, nor the men of the guard which followed me, none of us put off our clothes, saving that every one put them off for washing.* Nehemiah 4:23

At the end of a long day of work, the people just lay down in their work clothes for a few hours of rest, then rose up again to continue. These were serious people. Praise God!

As the work progressed, Nehemiah was faced with more challenges, from without and also from within. One day he discovered that certain men among the ruling class were taking advantage of the situation to charge high interest to their neighbors and friends, and he had to deal with their deceit.

> *Then I consulted with myself, and I rebuked the nobles, and the rulers, and said unto them, Ye exact usury, every one of his brother. And I set a great assembly against them.* Nehemiah 5:7

No sooner had that fire been put out than another erupted. Sanballat, having failed in his previous attempts to halt the work, now called upon Nehemiah to join him in a peace conference. Nehemiah sent his regrets, saying that he was too busy to attend.

> *And I sent messengers unto them, saying, I am doing a great work, so that I cannot come down: why should the work cease, whilst I leave it, and come down to you?*   Nehemiah 6:3

If you are doing something that God has commissioned you to do, what you are doing is a *"great work."* Don't let the devil hinder you. Don't stop for anything. Keep working.

Sanballat sent five delegations to Nehemiah, attempting to divert him and rob him of the time he needed to oversee the work. He knew that a work delayed is often a work unfinished. But, Nehemiah kept working.

From within, Shemaiah approached Nehemiah as a prophet and said that he knew of a plan to kill Nehemiah and that Nehemiah should hide in the temple. Nehemiah refused.

> *And I said, Should such a man as I flee? and who is there, that, being as I am, would go into the temple to save his life? I will not go in.*
> Nehemiah 6:11

Nehemiah learned that Sanballat had paid this man to try to trick him. When you want to do something for God, you have to keep your guard up all the time.

At last, after many such trials, and despite all the enemy's attempts to stop the work, it was finished.

> *So the wall was finished in the twenty and fifth day of the month Elul, in fifty and two days.*
> Nehemiah 6:15

It took only fifty-two days to accomplish such a daunting task. What a miracle! Isn't it amazing what we can do when we have a heart to work and leaders who keep us focused on the proper task!

Thus began a new and exciting chapter in the life of the people of God. If you will learn the importance of work, God will use you mightily for His glory.

- 12 -

LEARN TO AVOID SPIRITUAL BLINDNESS

PART I, THE CASE OF THE MAN BORN BLIND

And as Jesus passed by, he saw a man which was blind from his birth. And his disciples asked him, saying, Master, who did sin, this man, or his parents, that he was born blind? Jesus answered, Neither hath this man sinned, nor his parents: but that the works of God should be made manifest in him. John 9:1-3

Was it the sin of the man, himself, or the sin of his parents that caused him to be born blind?, the disciples reasoned.

Jesus responded that it wasn't the fault of either the man or his parents, but so that the *"works of God"* could be shown in this man, and He proceeded to heal him.

Sometimes, when Jesus performed His miracles, He told the people who witnessed them or who received them to keep it quiet and not tell a single person. This time was to be different. This particular healing raised quite a stir in the neighborhood.

Some of the neighbors were amazed because they knew that the man had been blind from birth. Others, however, were convinced that it could not be the same man. "He just looks like the blind man," they contended. It's really someone else.

The final word came from the man himself.

I am he.   John 9:9

When it became apparent that the man was telling the truth, the neighbors wanted to know how it was that a man born blind could suddenly see. Again, the answer was simple and straightforward.

> *A man that is called Jesus made clay, and anointed mine eyes, and said unto me, Go to the pool of Siloam, and wash: and I went and washed, and I received sight.*   John 9:11

"A man that is called Jesus" had done it. That's all it takes, no matter what the problem, what the need, or what the diagnosis might be. No matter if you are facing an impossibility in life, when *"a man that is*

called Jesus" gets involved, the problem is quickly resolved. When He is present, victory is assured.

Both puzzled and amazed, these neighbors then took the man in question before the Pharisees, and what followed presents one of the great courtroom dramas of the Bible.

That must have been an exciting scene. The townspeople were standing around waiting for details of the case to unfold. The former blind man was still visibly shaken by what had just happened to him. And, looking down from their pompous positions of authority, were several grim-faced Pharisaic officials.

They had received so many reports of miraculous healings done by this man Jesus that they were determined to get to the bottom of all this. They were tired of his chicanery. Too many people were fooled by his tricks. They would make a public example of this impostor and, once and for all, lay these false rumors to rest. They began their questioning.

"Tell us now, how is it you say you regained your sight?"

The man answered easily:

> *He put clay upon mine eyes, and I washed, and*
> *do see.* John 9:15

"That's impossible!" shouted one of the Pharisees. This man is not of God. If he were, he would honor the Sabbath, which he clearly did not do in dealing with you in this way."

"But, wait a minute," interrupted another. "If this man is a common sinner, how could he do a miracle as great as this one?" The questioners were divided on the issue themselves.

As they proceeded with their interrogation, they were unable to make the man change his story. They finally decided that he must be insane or a terrible liar and incapable of speaking for himself, so they called his parents in and questioned them.

"Now, look at this man carefully," the questioner demanded. "Are you sure that this man is your son whom you say was born blind?"

"We're sure," they answered. "That's our son."

"You're sure? There is no doubt in your mind?"

"We're sure."

"If this is your son, whom you claim was born blind, how do you account for the fact that this man is not blind, but sees?"

This question put the parents in a very difficult position. They had already received the notice that any person who admitted that Jesus was the Messiah would be put out of the synagogue. They didn't know what to say to these angry men. There must have been some stuttering and stammering going on and some whispered consultations, until, at last they hit upon the correct answer, one that would not jeopardize their stand in the community or in the synagogue.

"This is, without a doubt, our son," they said, "and he was born blind. Many of those who are present could testify to that fact. But how he is able to see we aren't sure. But, why not ask *him*? He is of age and can speak for himself."

With that, the former blind man was recalled to the stand and instructed by the court officials:

> *Give God the praise: we know that this man is a*
> *sinner.*   John 9:24

The simple answer the man gave them is a classic.

> *He answered and said, Whether he be a sinner or*
> *no, I know not: one thing I know, that, whereas I*
> *was blind, now I see.*   John 9:25

They judged Jesus to be a sinner simply because He didn't hesitate to heal a needy person on the Sabbath. The man who was healed recognized that he was incapable of judging whether that actually constituted a sin or not. He only knew that he could now see. That was enough.

The crowd, no doubt, was enjoying this battle of wits, happy that somebody would stand up to the Pharisees.

"Assuming that what you say is true," the questioner continued, "assuming that this Jesus did indeed open your eyes, what exactly did he say to you or do to you to produce this alleged miracle?"

"I told you once already," the man replied, "and you didn't seem to hear what I was saying. Why are you asking me again? Do you want to be His disciples too?"

I can imagine that an undercurrent of muffled snickering must have gone through the crowd at that point. They knew that becoming one of Jesus's disciples was the last thing the Pharisees had in mind. To the contrary, they were trying to find something they could use against Jesus, anything to keep people from believing Him and following Him.

Now, they were angered by the interruption. They were losing control of the situation and, therefore, lost their composure and begin to revile the man being questioned.

> *Then they reviled him, and said, Thou art his disciple; but we are Moses' disciples. We know that God spake unto Moses: as for this fellow, we know not from whence he is.*   John 9:28-29

They did not say it openly, but they were hinting at the rumors that Jesus was an illegitimate child. They were desperate now and were grasping at anything that could help them turn the people's attention away from Jesus.

In this moment, however, the man born blind received wonderful wisdom from God and answered in an amazing fashion.

> *The man answered and said unto them, Why herein is a marvellous thing, that ye know not from whence he is, and yet he hath opened mine eyes. Now we know that God heareth not sin-*

> *ners: but if any man be a worshipper of God, and*
> *doeth his will, him he heareth. Since the world*
> *began was it not heard that any man opened the*
> *eyes of one that was born blind. If this man were*
> *not of God, he could do nothing.*   John 9:30-33

This is powerful reasoning, and it answered well the major contentions of the Pharisees. The amazing thing about this answer is that blind people, in those days, were not well educated. The feeling was that they had little to offer in life. They were usually left to beg or to depend on their parents for the rest of their lives. It is logical to think that this man probably had little or no formal education, yet his words were very eloquent, and he spoke with great boldness. There can be no doubt that the man was inspired of the Holy Spirit to speak these words which quickly destroyed all the arguments of the Pharisees.

I can just imagine how the crowd reacted to all of this. Large numbers of them must have stood in utter amazement as they listened to such words of wisdom flowing from the lips of an unlearned man. And they must have held their breath with expectation of the explosion this response would provoke in the Pharisees.

That explosion was not long in coming.

> *They answered and said unto him, Thou wast*
> *altogether born in sins, and dost thou teach us?*
> *And they cast him out.*   John 9:34

The Pharisees were beside themselves. Pointing at the humble man who stood before them, they shouted and gesticulated, and when they could think of no more insults to hurl upon him or of any way to charge him further, they had him bodily thrown out.

Jesus heard what had happened and, considering what an ordeal this whole episode must have been for the former blind man, He went in search of the man to comfort him and draw him yet closer.

> *Jesus heard that they had cast him out; and when he had found him, he said unto him, Dost thou believe on the Son of God?*
> *He answered and said, Who is he, Lord, that I might believe on him?*
> *And Jesus said unto him, Thou hast both seen him, and it is he that talketh with thee.*
> *And he said, Lord, I believe. And he worshipped him.*
> *And Jesus said, For judgment I am come into this world, that they which see not might see; and that they which see might be made blind.*
> John 9:35-39

As Christians, each of us at some time or other in our Christian walk has felt cast out and unwanted, perhaps by those we loved the most. It is not unusual for family and friends to suddenly see us as enemies and to treat us accordingly. It is a very lonely feeling. But Jesus always finds us in such moments and comforts us and uses the circumstances to draw us closer to Himself.

This man's faith was far from perfect. Despite his eloquent defense of Jesus before the Pharisees, his knowledge of God was only in the beginning stages. Jesus led him deeper.

The statement Jesus then made may have been more for those who were within hearing distance than for the man himself. *"For judgment I am come into this world, that they which see not might see; and that they which see might be made blind."* If that was the case, it worked, for some Pharisees who were standing nearby observing the former blind man heard that and asked Jesus:

> *Are we blind also?* John 9:40

Jesus replied:

> *If ye were blind, ye should have no sin: but now ye say, We see; therefore your sin remaineth.*
> John 9:41

While the Pharisees intended to ask of physical blindness, Jesus answered the question spiritually. If they really did not understand what He had been teaching, then they were not guilty for rejecting it. They did understand, He was sure, and thus were guilty of rejecting His truths. Because they were sure that they already knew all truth, they had hardened their hearts against anything new. They were, therefore, spiritually blind and their sin remained.

May the Lord remove from each of us any spiritual blindness or inability to see His hand of mercy reaching out to us. Let us learn to listen carefully to the Lord, as little children, and to obey Him fully.

PART II, THE CASE OF THE DISCIPLES

Even the disciples of Jesus had to struggle with spiritual blindness, and Jesus spent time teaching them to avoid it, as He did one day as they were returning to Jerusalem.

> *And they were in the way going up to Jerusalem; and Jesus went before them: and they were amazed; and as they followed, they were afraid. And he took again the twelve, and began to tell them what things should happen unto him, Saying, Behold, we go up to Jerusalem; and the Son of man shall be delivered unto the chief priests, and unto the scribes; and they shall condemn him to death, and shall deliver him to the Gentiles: And they shall mock him, and shall scourge him, and shall spit upon him, and shall kill him: and the third day he shall rise again.*
>
> Mark 10:32-34

Jesus knew what lie ahead of Him and began giving them a vivid description of events that were to unfold in the days to come.

The disciples were *"amazed"* and *"afraid,"* amazed that Jesus was even willing to go to Jerusalem, since

He knew what He would face there, and afraid that they would somehow be caught up in the hatred many were displaying toward Him. His description of the events to come only heightened those fears. The love He felt for all mankind made suffering the cross and its consequences bearable for Jesus, but the disciple found it all very disquieting — to say the least. They were overwhelmed. That such a sacrifice was necessary on God's part was yet beyond their comprehension.

James and John changed the subject and asked a very mundane question of the Lord, a favor of sorts.

> *Grant unto us that we may sit, one on thy right hand, and the other on thy left hand, in thy glory.* Mark 10:37

Jesus had opened His heart to the disciples and described to them the deep secrets of His innermost being. He was about to give His life for the sins of others. He was about to place Himself as a sacrifice upon the altar of God and to extend to every man the opportunity to accept eternal life through His sacrifice. How absurd the request of the disciples must have seemed to Him at that moment!

Were the disciples blind to what Jesus was saying to them? Were they unable to catch the import of His words? How could they have asked such a "favor" at a moment like this? Jesus was about to fulfill the inspired words of John:

> *For God so loved the world, that he gave his only*
> *begotten Son, that whosoever believeth in him*
> *should not perish, but have everlasting life.*
>   John 3:16

At the same moment, the disciples were jockeying for position in the Kingdom. How carnal! How blind!

But men haven't changed much over the generations. Many of us are just like James and John. We sometimes argue with God about His will for us or we say to Him in prayer: "When are You going to hear my prayer, Lord? I have needs. Don't You care?"

How dare we ask the Lord if He cares! No one cares like He does. No one is capable of caring like He does. How dare we question God's love. He is love. No one can love like He loves.

> *He that loveth not knoweth not God; for God is*
> *love.*   1 John 4:8

What terrible blindness the disciples demonstrated that day!

We marvel that Jesus didn't give up on such men; but He didn't. He understands our limitations. He understands that those who are earthbound lack spiritual insight. With great tenderness He answered the request of the disciples.

> *To sit on my right hand and on my left hand is*
> *not mine to give; but it shall be given to them for*
> *whom it is prepared.*   Mark 10:40

Jesus set Himself up as the example of a servant to man and God.

> *For even the Son of man came not to be minis-*
> *tered unto, but to minister, and to give his life a*
> *ransom for many.*   Mark 10:45

As they continued on their way to Jerusalem, they came to Jericho where blind Bartimaeus sat by the roadside begging. When he heard that Jesus was coming, he began to cry out:

> *Jesus, thou Son of David, have mercy on me.*
>   Mark 10:47

Those who heard Bartimaeus cry out in this way tried to quiet him. Some things never change. People get upset when anyone shows excitement about Jesus. While it is considered normal to get hysterical at a football game, to shout yourself hoarse at a political rally, or to act the fool in a demonstration or a parade, religious observance must be conducted quietly — or so the world thinks. Hallelujahs and amens disturb those who would prefer to sleep through a sermon.

Thank God that Bartimaeus didn't know the church regulations. He wasn't aware of the fact that he needed to please religious leaders. All he knew was that he had a need and that Jesus was passing by. He got excited because he realized that this was his day for a miracle. So, when those around him tried to quiet him, he shouted louder, until Jesus heard and responded.

And Jesus stood still, and commanded him to be called. And they call the blind man, saying unto him, Be of good comfort, rise; he calleth thee. And he, casting away his garment, rose, and came to Jesus. And Jesus answered and said unto him, What wilt thou that I should do unto thee? The blind man said unto him, Lord, that I might receive my sight. And Jesus said unto him, Go thy way; thy faith hath made thee whole. And immediately he received his sight, and followed Jesus in the way.   Mark 10:49-52

As difficult as it can be to face life handicapped by physical blindness, spiritual blindness is a much worse handicap. Bartimaeus was physically blind, but spiritually he saw his opportunity. His faith inspired Jesus to ask him what he wanted. That must have seemed like a very strange question to those who heard it. Wasn't it obvious that the man was blind and needed his sight? It may have been obvious, but Jesus wanted Bartimaeus to declare his need with his own lips because this would help his faith to receive the miracle he needed.

Ye have not, because ye ask not.   James 4:2

We must *"boldly"* make our requests known unto the Lord.

Let us therefore come boldly unto the throne of grace, that we may obtain mercy, and find grace to help in time of need. Hebrews 4:16

When Bartimaeus had declared his need, Jesus' response was simple and direct: *"Go thy way; thy faith hath made thee whole."* And, when Bartimaeus had *"received his sight,"* he *"followed Jesus in the way."* What a wonderful example for us to follow!

As the disciples who had been with Jesus for more than three years, demonstrated spiritual blindness, a poor beggar had his eyes opened and became a follower of Christ. Let us pray that the Lord will open the eyes of each one of us, to see as He sees, to understand as He understands, and to know as He knows. Let us become aware of God's undying love and concern for each of us, everyday, in every situation of life. Learn to avoid spiritual blindness. 📖

- 13 -

LEARN THE SOURCE OF
ALL KNOWLEDGE AND POWER

Then he called his twelve disciples together, and gave them power and authority over all devils, and to cure diseases. And he sent them to preach the kingdom of God, and to heal the sick. And he said unto them, Take nothing for your journey, neither staves, nor scrip, neither bread, neither money; neither have two coats apiece. And whatsoever house ye enter into, there abide, and thence depart. And whosoever will not receive you, when ye go out of that city, shake off the very dust from your feet for a testimony against them. And they departed, and went through the towns, preaching the gospel, and healing every where. Luke 9:1-6

Jesus sent His disciples out to put into practice what He had been teaching them. They were not sent, however, in their own strength. He *"gave them power and authority."*

They went out with specific instructions concerning what they were to do, where they were to go and what they were to take with them. He told them to stay in the place provided for them by the local people. This may seem insignificant to some, but Jesus wanted His disciples to concentrate on the ministry and not be bothered about details that could distract them.

When the disciples returned, they reported to Jesus everything that had happened on this journey.

> *And the apostles, when they were returned, told him all that they had done. And he took them, And went aside privately into a desert place belonging to the city called Bethsaida.*
>
> Luke 9:10

I find the phrase *"all that they had done"* a little alarming because I know that the tendency of men and women everywhere is to forget that our power comes from God and to begin thinking that we have actually accomplished something on our own. He gave them power. They had no power of their own.

We must be careful to give the Lord glory for the things He does in us and through us. He said:

> *And I, if I be lifted up from the earth, will draw all men unto me.*   John 12:32

After the disciples had briefed Jesus on their activities, He took them aside to teach them more. We never know it all, and no matter how far we have come in our Christian experience, there is a lot more to learn.

These men would continue the work of Jesus after He had returned to Heaven. They would establish the New Testament Church and produce the New Testament Scriptures. They had a LOT to learn. But others had discovered where Jesus was going and had followed Him, hoping to receive His blessing.

And the people, when they knew it, followed him: and he received them, and spake unto them of the kingdom of God, and healed them that had need of healing. Luke 9:11

It was now late in the day and the disciples became anxious about how they would feed this great multitude of people. They thought it would be better to send them away before mealtime, but Jesus had something else in mind. He turned the tables on them and commanded:

Give ye them to eat. Luke 9:13

The disciples were stunned by this command. They couldn't do that, they said. They had so little themselves. How could they feed such a great crowd? They were looking at the crowd and not at the Lord who could supply all things. He had given them *"power and authority."* They just hadn't learned yet all that could be done with that power.

When you insist on looking at the problem instead of the Problem Solver, the problem will only get bigger and bigger. If you continue to look at the problem, your faith will only get smaller and smaller.

They didn't know it yet, but the Lord was preparing them for the next phase of their ministry. They had to recognize the power they already possessed. They couldn't have power to do something unless they *believed* they had the power to do it. And how would they know if they had the power to do it if they didn't first try? Jesus was teaching them that when something seemed impossible they were to call on Him and know that He would do what they were asking.

> *Then he took the five loaves and the two fishes, and looking up to heaven, he blessed them, and brake, and gave to the disciples to set before the multitude.*   Luke 9:16

He gave to them, and they were to give to others. They were only giving out what had been given to them. And it worked. Everyone present was fed, and there were twelve basketfuls left over. Why twelve basketfuls? Perhaps one basketful was for each apostle, to help each one overcome his doubts.

When the crowd finally dispersed, Jesus sat down with His apostles and asked them some more personal questions.

Whom say the people that I am?   Luke 9:18

When the disciples reported what they had heard, His next question was, What do you think?

But whom say ye that I am?   Luke 9:20

Peter's famous answer was:

The Christ of God.   Luke 9:20

This was not a frivolous question, and Peter could not give a frivolous answer. Each of us must ask ourselves, Who is Jesus to me? And each of us must meditate on the answer. He is, we know, our Creator, our Savior, our Healer, the Promised One, the One on whom our future depends. Keeping our focus on Him will help us face what each and every tomorrow may hold.

Next, Jesus shared with them some of the secrets of His heart.

The Son of man must suffer many things, and be rejected of the elders and chief priests and scribes, and be slain, and be raised the third day.
Luke 9:22

They must know the price He would pay because of His love for all mankind. After He let these thoughts sink in for a while, He continued:

And he said to them all, If any man will come after me, let him deny himself, and take up his cross daily, and follow me. For whosoever will save his life shall lose it: but whosoever will lose his life for my sake, the same shall save it.

Luke 9:23-24

Now they must seriously consider their commitment to the Lord and determine how willing they were to follow Him, come what may.

The disciples must have been breathless with all that they were learning. Who could have blamed them if they had felt they simply could not take it all in? While they were still thinking about what it would cost to follow the Lord, Jesus took Peter, James and John and went up into a high mountain to pray. This would not have seemed unusual, for they often prayed together; but something unusual was about to happen. Jesus was about to be transfigured before their eyes. And two other men appeared and spoke with Him, two men from the past.

And as he prayed, the fashion of his countenance was altered, and his raiment was white and glistering. And, behold, there talked with him two men, which were Moses and Elias: Who appeared in glory, and spake of his decease which he should accomplish at Jerusalem.

Luke 9:29-31

The natural scene was replaced by a supernatural one. Why did Moses and Elijah appear on the mountain? The scriptures say that they spoke to Jesus *"of his decease."* The coming events were, no doubt, heavy on the heart of Jesus, but it was difficult for Him to discuss it with the disciples, for they could not fully grasp what was to take place. In fact, when the glory of the men of the past appeared on the mountain, the disciples had fallen asleep and witnessed the glory only when the glow of it woke them up.

> *But Peter and they that were with him were heavy with sleep: and when they were awake, they saw his glory, and the two men that stood with him.* Luke 9:32

"They saw His glory." You have to wake up to see it. You have to rouse yourself out of stupor to realize His will for your life. You may just sleep through all the greatest blessings. If you have been distracted by something else, if you have become involved in something that is taking your attention away from the glorious thing God is doing in the earth, if you are looking for attention or recognition, for open doors of opportunity in ministry, or for someone to meet your needs, you will surely miss seeing His glory.

Wake up, Church. See His glory. See His power. See His hand of blessing. See His wisdom. See His deliverance.

When Peter was finally able to speak, he said:

> *Master, it is good for us to be here: and let us*
> *make three tabernacles; one for thee, and one for*
> *Moses, and one for Elias: not knowing what he*
> *said.*   Luke 9:33

"It is good to be here." He was correct in that statement, but his next conclusions were in error. He
thought they should do something, make something,
get involved in the situation. He was so excited that
he really didn't know what he was saying.

I can understand that. We often do the same thing.
We get inspired and want to start doing something,
anything. We want to be active and involved. We
want to go somewhere, anywhere. But this is not
God's way.

His instructions are specific, not just, 'Do something.' He requires a specific thing. He doesn't say,
'Go somewhere, anywhere.' He has a specific place
where He can use us now.

In moments like these, instead of making all sorts
of plans, we just need to get quiet and wait before the
Lord so that He can teach us and reveal all His will to
us. If nothing else, we need time, just to know Him in
all His glory.

Too often we are looking for results, whereas He is
looking for our attention, our surrendered heart, our
obedience, our listening ear. That is more important
to Him than any earthly temple we could build for
His glory.

Peter, James and John were such privileged individuals to be chosen as witnesses of this awesome

scene, the revelation of the glory of the Lord. But they have nothing on us. We have the privilege and opportunity to come into God's presence daily and to stand in His glory as they did. What blessed people we are!

The glory of God came down over the mountain like a cloud, and out of the midst of the glory came a voice.

> *While he thus spake, there came a cloud, and overshadowed them: and they feared as they entered into the cloud. And there came a voice out of the cloud, saying, This is my beloved Son: hear him.*   Luke 9:34-35

God was saying to the disciples, "Forget about your building plans and learn to listen to the Words of My Son. They are Words of eternal life that will give meaning to your existence. You must submit all to His will for your life."

The scene shifts once again, and the group comes down the mountain.

> *And it came to pass, that on the next day, when they were come down from the hill, much people met him.*   Luke 9:37

You can be sure that those men would have loved to stay right there on the mountain top. That is exactly what Peter had in mind when he suggested the building of the three tabernacles. We would all like to stay in the glory of God permanently. But there comes a time in our lives when we have to come down from the mountain to minister to people. We go to the mountain to get filled with God's power and wisdom, but we cannot stay there indefinitely. We must come down, so that we can give out what we have received to others. As Jesus said:

> *Heal the sick, cleanse the lepers, raise the dead, cast out devils: freely ye have received, freely give.*   Matthew 10:8

The gifts and abilities that God gives are not for self aggrandizement. They are to be given away, to be shared with others, to be poured out. Love is not love until it is shared.

Among the crowd that met them that day for ministry was a desperate father, bringing his son for ministry. He first spoke with the disciples, but they were unable to help him. Jesus sparked faith in the man's heart when He said, *"Bring thy son hither"* (Luke 9:41). That's the answer to everyone who needs a miracle. Mother and Dad don't have all the answers. Doctors and medicine can't always help. They are greatly limited. Money can't always buy what we need. Even governments can't solve many of the world's problems. Come to Jesus. He has the answer. This was not a difficult case for Him.

> *And as he was yet a coming, the devil threw him down, and tare him. And Jesus rebuked the un-clean spirit, and healed the child, and delivered*

him again to his father. And they were all amazed at the mighty power of God. But while they wondered every one at all things which Jesus did, he said unto his disciples,
                                                                   Luke 9:42-43

Jesus had to continually reeducate His disciples. Just when He thought they were beginning to comprehend His message, they would begin to bicker over some trivial matter.

Let these sayings sink down into your ears: for the Son of man shall be delivered into the hands of men. But they understood not this saying, and it was hid from them, that they perceived it not: and they feared to ask him of that saying. Then there arose a reasoning among them, which of them should be greatest.
                                                                   Luke 9:44-46

To answer them, Jesus set a child before them.

And Jesus, perceiving the thought of their heart, took a child, and set him by him, And said unto them, Whosoever shall receive this child in my name receiveth me: and whosoever shall receive me receiveth him that sent me: for he that is least among you all, the same shall be great.
                                                                   Luke 9:47-48

As they continued on their way to Jerusalem, they passed by Samaria. But they were not well received

there. This angered the disciples and they felt that
something must be done. James and John, considering the new powers they were experiencing (and
remembering the example of Elisha and the 450
prophets of Baal), suggested that they call fire down
from heaven upon these people. This brought a
strong rebuke from the Master.

> *But he turned, and rebuked them, and said, Ye
> know not what manner of spirit ye are of. For the
> Son of man is not come to destroy men's lives,
> but to save them. And they went to another vil-
> lage.*   Luke 9:55-56

Finally, they met several people who had their
own ideas about serving the Lord.

> *And it came to pass, that, as they went in the
> way, a certain man said unto him, Lord, I will
> follow thee whithersoever thou goest. And Jesus
> said unto him, Foxes have holes, and birds of the
> air have nests; but the Son of man hath not
> where to lay his head. And he said unto another,
> Follow me. But he said, Lord, suffer me first to
> go and bury my father. Jesus said unto him, Let
> the dead bury their dead: but go thou and preach
> the kingdom of God. And another also said,
> Lord, I will follow thee; but let me first go bid
> them farewell, which are at home at my house.
> And Jesus said unto him, No man, having put*

his hand to the plough, and looking back, is fit
for the kingdom of God.   Luke 9:57-62

Jesus made it clear to each of these individuals
what we must each learn: serving God means serving God. It must be done in His way. He will accept
no other. He is our Source of all power, knowledge,
wisdom, and authority. Each of us must learn it well.

📖

- 14 -

LEARN TO BE FAITHFUL

And, behold, men brought in a bed a man which was taken with a palsy: and they sought means to bring him in, and to lay him before him. And when they could not find by what way they might bring him in because of the multitude, they went upon the housetop, and let him down through the tiling with his couch into the midst before Jesus.

And when he saw their faith, he said unto him, Man, thy sins are forgiven thee.

And the scribes and the Pharisees began to reason, saying, Who is this which speaketh blasphemies? Who can forgive sins, but God alone?

> *But when Jesus perceived their thoughts, he an-*
> *swering said unto them, What reason ye in your*
> *hearts? Whether is easier, to say, Thy sins be*
> *forgiven thee; or to say, Rise up and walk? But*
> *that ye may know that the Son of man hath*
> *power upon earth to forgive sins, (he said unto*
> *the sick of the palsy,) I say unto thee, Arise, and*
> *take up thy couch, and go into thine house.*
> *And immediately he rose up before them, and*
> *took up that whereon he lay, and departed to his*
> *own house, glorifying God. And they were all*
> *amazed, and they glorified God, and were filled*
> *with fear, saying, We have seen strange things*
> *to day.*   Luke 5:18-26

What a wonderful story of determination! And these are not prophets or apostles or kings. These are everyday laymen.

Jesus had entered a certain house and was seated in the midst of a large crowd of people who had gathered to hear His teachings. And there are five other principal characters in the story: a very sick man and his four friends who had determined to get him to Jesus so that he could be healed and who were, even now, on their way to this house where Jesus was teaching, carrying their friend on a stretcher.

The Bible says nothing about how far these men carried the man or what other obstacles they might have encountered along the way. We don't know what time of day it was or how hot it might have been at the time or whether it was raining hard. Ap-

parently, none of that mattered. These men were determined to get their friend to Jesus — whatever the
circumstances.

It couldn't have been easy to carry a very sick man
across the arid and rocky lands or through the streets
of the city, and when they came within sight of the
house where Jesus was, they must have felt relief.

They soon saw, however, that the crowd had
grown so large that the doors and windows were all
blocked, hopelessly jammed with eager people, each
one wanting to get closer to Jesus, to hear His voice
or even to touch Him. There was no way they could
wrestle a stretcher through that mass of humanity.
Their way was blocked.

The devil must have laughed and tried to get these
men to turn around and go home. I can imagine that
he said something like this:

> You've done your best for your friend, but
> there's no way you'll ever be able to get to see the
> Master today. And you must think of your
> friend. He is, after all, a very sick man. The Lord
> is pleased with your willingness to try to help
> him, but it is impossible under these circum-
> stances. You'll just have to go back home and try
> another time.

It would have been very easy to agree with this
kind of thinking, and most of us might have given up
and tried another day — if the man lived long
enough. But these men did not give up easily. They
had determined to be a blessing to the sick man, and

they were not about to disappoint him now. But what could they do? Well, there is always a way — when we are determined to find it.

Looking over the situation carefully, these man saw a possibility that others might have overlooked. If they could somehow get the stretcher up onto the rooftop, it might be possible to remove enough of the tiles to lower him down from above. It just might work. They had to try.

Many of us, instead of thinking of the good things that could result from such a daring venture, instead of picturing the sick man in the presence of Jesus, healed and rejoicing, would succumb to thoughts of all the things that could go wrong. How terrible it would be to slip and let the man fall and be injured or killed! How terrible it would be to incur the wrath of the owner of the house for taking the roof apart! How terrible it would be if Jesus were angry for being interrupted in the middle of His teaching! Some of us waste our lives thinking about all the terrible things that *might* happen, and, as a consequence, we seldom take daring steps.

Faith makes you bold, and faith makes you determined. If you believe that God is going to do a miracle, you don't easily give up or become discouraged — whatever the circumstances. These men were convinced that they could do this thing, and they set about to finish the job they had begun.

The scene then changes, and we look inside the house. The Master is intently blessing the people with His words. There is a look of anticipation on the faces of those who listen. There are some sick people present, and they can hardly wait for the teaching to end so that they can ask Jesus to heal them. Then, suddenly, some ropes are seen dangling from the ceiling, and a stretcher with a feeble-looking man on it drops down in front of the Lord.

What the Bible says at this point is so significant: *"When He saw their faith ..."* It was the determined faith of the four friends that brought the sick man to Jesus and to healing and a new life. Their faith made them willing to use extraordinary means to accomplish the task. They did not give up simply because there was an obstacle. They did not give up simply because the task was not an easy one. They did what was necessary. They brought their friend to Jesus.

Jesus first said unto him, *"Man, thy sins are forgiven."* The friends may have been motivated to their heroic action by the sickness of the man's body, but they had the underlying hope that he would be transformed in his soul, as well. He needed Jesus, they knew. Now, their faith was rewarded.

This brought a strong response from the scribes and Pharisees. They considered this to be *"blasphemy."* After all, *"who can forgive sins but God alone?"*

Then Jesus told the man to do three things:

1. Arise.
2. Take up your bed.
3. Walk.

Jesus manifested His supernatural power, but the sick man had to do something to show his willingness to submit to Jesus as Lord of His life. He had to show faith for himself. He had to act in some way. In this case, it was to get up, pick up his stretcher, and carry it home.

If he had, at this moment, allowed his reasoning mind to control his actions, he would never have received the miracle. After all, he had been sick for a very long time, and, no doubt, there was not much strength left in his body. It would have been easy to think that he could not get up, could not pick up the stretcher, and could not carry it home. If he had reached this conclusion and had failed to act on the Lord's words, he would have remained where he was.

But determined faith is catching. If these men had gone to all this trouble, they must know something. When you project a positive faith, others will be affected by it.

The Lord had commanded three things, and the man did those three things *"immediately."*

1. He rose up before them.
2. He took up that whereon he lay.
3. He departed to his own house.

And, all the while, he was *"glorifying God."*

It all happened so quickly, so easily. And great miracles are waiting for you. If you have determined faith, if you will make up your mind not to give up, not to become discouraged when you face difficulties, not to stop until you have finished your mission, the Lord will make a way for you. Learn to be faithful.

- 15 -

EVER LEARNING

Ever learning, and never able to come to the knowledge of the truth.   2 Timothy 3:7

There are people, as we see from this biblical passage, who are *"ever learning"* yet *"never able to come to the knowledge of the truth."* This has led many to believe that learning is not a spiritual pursuit and that it is better to be ignorant. Nothing in the Scriptures confirms this thought; and it is sad to see many Christians wasting their lives, incapable of being effective for the Lord, incapable of being a blessing to others, incapable of reaching out to the lost, lifting up the fallen, and ministering to sick and suffering people, simply because they have been robbed of the benefits of the basic lessons of Christian life.

Although we certainly do not want to be as those who are *"ever learning"* yet *"never able to come to the knowledge of the truth,"* we do want to continue to learn more and more so that we can do more and more for our Savior and Lord. Learning is not just for children or young people. I am learning new things every day, sitting daily at the Lord's banqueting table, and I find that His wisdom and knowledge never run out. Until we get to heaven, where we will *know as we are known*, we must never stop learning. There can, therefore, never be a final chapter for us on earth, just as God Himself, and His Word are eternal. His truth never ends, and His willingness and desire to teach us will never change.

Our heavenly Father always has one more course prepared for us. He always has one more revelation to open to us, one more mystery to reveal to us. His Word is always fresh, always new. When we go deeper, we find that it is still deeper and when we go higher, we find that it is still higher.

God is still working with His people, still molding His Church, still preparing His Bride. The Acts of the Apostles has not been completed, but continues to be played out across the world — wherever men and women dare to believe God and to accept His call to service.

Let us consider carefully the things we have learned. Personally, I am overwhelmed by the variety of teaching given in the Bible, by the variety of styles used by the various authors, and yet by the continuity of the story of God's marvelous works, from creation to final redemption. It is His desire to make us more like Him so that we might shed forth His light to the world around us.

It won't be long now until the final judgments begin to fall and until Satan, our enemy, will be exposed, once and for all, for the paper tiger he is, a bully destined for defeat. It won't be long now before he and his crowd will be cast into the Lake of Fire. Then, after all the battles and struggles of the ages have ceased, we will reach our goal: to be present with the Lord forever.

What a great word!

Forever!

Forever!

Forever!

Forever!

We will never tire of saying it, throughout eternity.

Forever ... with the Lord!

Having learned many new lessons of faith and per-severance, we are now more convinced than ever that nothing and nobody else but Jesus can satisfy the longing within our hearts. And, together, we say, with John the Revelator:

Even so, come, Lord Jesus.   Revelation 22:20

Amen!